LIBRARY SYSTEMS AND INFORMATION SERVICES

Proceedings of the second Anglo-C~

Conference of Information S:

Edited by
D. J. FOSKETT, M. A., F.L.A.
A. de REUCK, M. Sc.
H. COBLANS, Ph. D.

ARCHON BOOKS

HAMDEN CONNECTICUT

PRINTED IN GREAT BRITAIN

LIBRARY SYSTEMS AND INFORMATION SERVICES

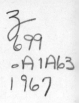

CONTENTS

v

INTRODUCTION

This book contains the Proceedings of the second Anglo-Czech Conference of Information Specialists, which was held in London in 1967. It was organised jointly by Aslib, OSTI, and the Ciba Foundation, with the close co-operation of the Centre for Scientific, Technical and Economic Information, Prague. The first conference, published by COSTEI in 1967, was held in Prague in 1966, and was intended to give the participants a general view of the information and library scene in the two countries. The second continued with fewer and more detailed accounts of specific services, some of which have not been widely reported before, and some not at all. This is the first time, for example, that most of the Czech services have been described for publication in English, though their methods are extremely up-to-date and have much to teach us in the West.

It is naturally disappointing that a number of unforeseen difficulties prevented publication sooner. The editors have felt, however, that we should proceed in spite of this, because we are sure that our colleagues in Western countries will be glad to have the opportunity to learn the details of some very impressive systems. All those who attended the meeting greatly appreciated the opportunity to exchange views between Czech and British colleagues and welcome this means of sharing the occasion with others unable to be present.

We should like to thank the organisers of the Conference, and, in particular, the Ciba Foundation, whose generous support made the conference possible. We should also like to thank Mr. Humphrey Wilson, our publisher, who has given us valuable advice and indeed made this publication possible.

While these papers were in the press, news came from Prague of the sudden tragic death of the leader of the Czech party, Dr. Bohumir Buncl. Known to all of us as "Papa", he left an indelible impression by his calm efficiency and his warm and lovable personality. We should like this volume to stand as a salute to his memory.

D.J.F.
A.V.S. de R.
H.C.

MANAGEMENT OF INFORMATION SERVICES IN CZECHOSLOVAKIA

BOHUMIR BUNCL

COSTEI, Prague

Some time ago Mr Anthony de Reuck made a statement to the effect that information services are an expensive matter and that society cannot expect to acquire information cheaply. I presume that this bitter truth is one of the bonds which are beginning to form between British and Czechoslovak information experts. In the course of the Small Meeting of Czechoslovak and British Information Specialists, in which some of you took part last year, we all made it clear that both of our countries have neither as much available money as the United States of America, nor so many organizational possibilities as the USSR, as to be able to secure widespread and to a considerable extent costly automated information systems. We cannot nor are we intending to organize information as a self-contained activity, a kind of bibliographic application of *l'art pour l'art.* Quite the contrary, for in our case as in yours, not only the cost of information but also the economical advantages arising from its application in practice, are very closely observed providing of course that we manage to find an effective way of revealing them.

You will recall the short exposé of Mr Guth, the vice president of the Centre for Scientific, Technical and Economic Information which was given last year at Liblice and is included in the Proceedings of that Meeting. There was nothing more to state at that time. The Centre had only been founded on April 1st, i.e. two months previous to our Small Meeting. Up to today, the body can pride itself on one year of life.

This one year has meant much to our country. The principles of our new economic system have been systematically introduced into the national economy. The development of science and technology and the exploitation of their results in production is becoming a decisive factor for the further growth of productivity of social work. Financial funds for science are increasing steadily in the whole world and naturally the same applies to our country as well. The cycle of doubling the size of staff on scientific and research activities practically coincides with the world average of ten to twelve years, but it more or less surpasses this average due to our situation in World War II, when under the German Occupation our scientific and research potential was nearly extinguished. The natural result was an increasing demand for information. The responsible authorities have realized that in technology as well as in science we cannot do without information or with information which is incomplete or gained at random. The importance of systematic information work is proved by such facts as for example that in the engineering branch Czechoslovakia produces about 70% of the world assortment, whereas the corresponding scientific and research basis represents only about 1% of the world total. We have realized that it is necessary to build up a system capable of furnishing this production with Scientific, Technical and Economic Information (STEI). It became evident that any tendency to save costs in the sphere of information was uneconomical, because this forced saving would cost us many times more in the form of uselessly repeated research. It would result in the discovery of things already discovered not only all over the world but possibly in our own country too, in the solving of problems already solved elsewhere, in noneffective and out-of-date production, in products of an overall inferior quality which are unacceptable to world markets and unfit even for home consumption etc.

For all these reasons our endeavour received political help. In the conclusions of the 13th Congress of the Communist Party of Czechoslovakia it was expressly formulated that it was necessary "to finish and improve the STEI system and to take a more effective part in the processing of information concerning the world of science." A necessity therefore arose to work out a realistic conception with a sufficient carrying capacity for the organization and function of an information network with the following mission:

To create facilities for information work assessing technical and economic conceptions by means of research, and analytical activity by elaborating complex comparative reviews showing the level of our and world technology.

To serve the needs of forming a draft plan for the development of science and technology and establishing tasks for research, development and preproduction up to the material realization as such; it must further serve the needs of inventive endeavour, the formation and introduction of standards and the improvement of individual personal qualification.

To offer adequate and satisfactory information for the needs of economy management, which is capable of evaluating the differences in data, in the sources of information, so that the data provided are comparable in form and usable by the management.

The development of the information system has acquired a clear aim:

To reach as soon as possible such a state where the information system would at the appropriate time furnish our economy and all its branches in advance with necessary information from home and foreign sources, viz. not only for the problems and tasks of national economy, but also for operational management.

At the same time it became clear that there was still a large number of experts for information work and that the existing team was losing time and capacity in dealing with less important details and tasks. For this reason we consider it necessary to concentrate our information work rather on the satisfying of such information demands as arise from the leading branches of our national economy, and chiefly on the needs of our state plan of development of science and technology. In the course of establishing the individual types of information centres it will be necessary to maintain a differential aspect and a highly differential providing of information to individual users according to their needs.

A quick rise in quality of information services demands a concentration of capacities and a concentration of staff for securing a good functioning of the most important information centres.

The new system of management of our national economy in itself evokes the necessity of a more intensive support to the improvement of our information services, especially where interdisciplinary relations are concerned. Because of this we have concentrated our attention on the following problems:

In the whole system we are continuously establishing three kinds of centres viz. primary, branch and disciplinary information centres. This communication pattern of scientific, technical and economic information is being completed and gradually materialized in the central management.

As a basic conception we are developing the informational follow-up of material problems via disciplinary and interdisciplinary relations. With respect to this basic conception it is essential to cover proportionally the information branches and science sections from the system to the user and maintain a feed back from such places, where information is prepared, back into the system.

It is necessary to secure the important links with the system of scientific and technical propaganda, chiefly with the press but also with means of state propaganda, i.e. radio and TV, which may be of great help to the information expert. Further it is necessary to form direct links with other parts of the national economy, and with individual systems which are directly connected with and inseparable from the information network, e.g. the system of libraries and the system of patent offices, which are closely connected with the information network by the character of their work.

Information work as such also deserves study and analysis. According to the above it is necessary to make the function, organization and technology of information services more precise, and to secure a gradual organisational transition to an integrated and mechanized system. To this purpose will serve research and development in the sphere of information work, and consistent personal verification of results, which are achieved in all the centres of the system covering the individual disciplines.

It is however no easy task to form conditions for raising the level of information centres by providing for staff, material and financial funds and their actual operation. That means not only forming a certain number, however large, of information centres, but also unifying them and forming a mutually inter-linked system, which would become more and more important to national economy.

This is the rough conception of the development of our information system, which serves as guide for our work in practice. This conception, which is gradually being introduced into practice, will be realized as follows:

In the function of the central organ for management and coordination of the nationwide information system and simultaneously as its main link will remain the Centre for Scientific, Technical and Economic Information. It unites the management and coordination of this system with the research of progressive information technology processes and further with the top interdisciplinary and sectional information activity. With respect to concentration of the necessary capacity it will be essential to deal with the existing lack of unity. For this reason the disciplinary information centres (centres of the first category) are to be established preferentially. They are not organized in accordance with the administrative structure, i.e. according to the organization of the central management, but from the material viewpoint, and they are to coordinate and secure the information concerning the whole discipline. I shall try to make this point more clear by means of the following example: The disciplinary centre for transport should possess a central documentation record, and secure information pertaining to railway transport, aeroplane, river-ship transport, truck and car transport, the construction and maintenance of city transport, the construction of roads and highways, regardless of which ministry is in administrative charge of the specific type of transport. These centres will be the information strongholds of the system in regulating the flow of information and at the same time they will be partners of the central management in the course of the actual application of this information. For the quicker furnishing of users with information and mainly because our possibilities are so far limited, we shall first of all establish approximately 100 – 120 centres of the second category from branch centres which secure information from the important leading branches, and at the same time establish socially important tasks. Centres of the first and second categories will form the authorized (or state) network, which owing to its nationwide importance will be financed from the state budget. Finances will be dealt with in greater detail by Mr Stefanik in his paper.

The information system will also make full use of regional centres (State scientific libraries in individual regions, bibliographic centres, houses of technology etc.) Thus a system of information centres open to the public will be formed, together with its own fundamental information holdings (libraries, records etc.)

As you will hear later, especially from the paper of Mr Dorský, an integrated system will be gradually built up with the use of computers. In the course of preparing for automation we intend to start with a pilot plant and gradually to enlarge operational processing on the basis of a unified organizational, technological and professional approach.

Our final aim is to form a unified information system which would cover the system of public information centres — such as for example state scientific libraries of public character — as well as the information system in industry and research, i.e. the information system of a more private character (production, applied research in industry, basic research in the Czechoslovak Academy of Science).

The formation and establishment of such an information system is connected with other problems which need working out in greater detail.

Between disciplinary centres and the central management, useful collaboration and labour division must take place in the process of forming information holdings and in their use. This also means a partnership in the solving and fulfilling of all problems. In directing the flow of information, the disciplinary centres represent a useful measure of suitable centralization in contrast to the present far too extensive growth of branch centres and in contrast to the existing extremely decentralized documentation activity. This will secure the advance to far more intensive information work in the future. Thus the central management will be able to keep at the centre only such a range of work, which it will be able to establish effectively. This relates not only to the forming of centralized stores and centrally directed information activity, but also to the direction of the complete information network itself.

From this point of view this relation represents a useful measure of centralization and decentralization in the management and direction of the whole system.

The Centre for Scientific, Technical and Economic Information already fulfils its functions by an operative contact with the network, by verifying and directing its function especially in wide cooperation with disciplinary centres, often through their direct intermediary. A further help in the management of the integrated system and in its forming is our endeavour to introduce complex mechanization and automation. And further there is the use of economic impulses, the regulation of financial and other means, the preparation of nationwide measures, securing of necessary expert studies and analyses, measures for the training of workers, of a sufficient supply of foreign information sources and the overall machine or material technical equipment. Often I have stated on various occasions that we can and will aim at directing a system such as this not just for the mere reason that a Government Decree or Act of Parliament has been passed, or that it is a momentary tendency, but because we shall render the system such services that this system will find it worthwhile to let itself be managed by us.

From the above it follows that:

It will be necessary to secure a system of grants for a noninvestment activity as a help mainly in the transitional period before all the consequences of the new system of economic management of the national economy will become manifest; to make the economic relations gradually felt where it would be reasonable in the interest of national economy. Perspectively we take it for granted that it will be necessary to secure the influence of the information system predominantly from the balance and in the form of grants. Especially it will be necessary to count on a relatively high cost of securing the mechanization and automation, and of establishing respective capacities for the function of a complex automated information system.

It will be necessary to secure the supply and communication of our own and also of foreign information sources. An increase of buying possibilities is reckoned with so as to render available the necessary number of information sources. However, we intend to solve and put into effect a systematic record of these imported sources and we want to have an account of their use and distribution. We consider to what extent the processing of world production is economical in our country and to what extent we shall make use of the available index journals in accordance with special conditions in the individual disciplines.

To secure the training of well prepared workers in the profession itself at specialized schools and to substantially improve their qualification structure in the system. This of course is closely connected with the appropriate rewarding of these workers. The material and technical basis of the whole system must be improved in the same way.

These and other measures will be realized in such a manner that they will enable the users of information to obtain quick and good information sources in research as well as in development, in projection and in the production cycle, in the setting up of long-term technical and economic proposals and in solving concrete tasks. A qualitative change in the portion of the information system in the further development of the national economy is unthinkable without systematic support given to the system and without substantial material help.

On the basis of our own and foreign experience it is beginning to appear that the complicated problem of STEI automation has to be solved step by step, viz. in the form of realization of partial projects; these projects will on the one hand gradually rationalize the information processes, and on the other hand will verify the progressive methodology and the need of machine equipment, so that at the end of the first period (i.e. 1970) realistic preconditions will have been created (i.e. software and hardware) for the function of the information system in the selected key information centres.

The creating of an effective mechanized and automated information system presupposes the solving of a number of problems which are dealt with in greater detail in the paper of Mr Dorský.

It will of course be necessary to realize all essential measures for securing qualified workers in the sphere of analysis, programming and managing of the technological process in the processing of information.

At the beginning of my paper I promised to tell you something about what we have managed during the short period of time which has elapsed between your visit in Czechoslovakia and our stay here. As soon as I got to the analysing of proposed work, which we have finished in this period, I could not possibly refrain from informing you about what we prepare for the immediate future.

I would like to give you a short review of the present situation, so that we can all realize what yet remains to be done for the successful realization of our long-term proposals.

You know some of the material and technical basis and you can form an idea about the buildings in which we work and about their mechanical equipment. You have seen our State Technical Library with its basic holdings located in Klementinum. This is a beautiful historical building, one of the marvels of Prague architecture; it is, however, an old cloister and not a modern practical building of the kind of which about two hundred have been built all over Europe during about the past thirty five years.

Projects of new buildings are planned, we have a building site together with the Czechoslovak Academy of Science and we hope within a relatively not very distant time to be able to pride ourselves with a new building, where the whole COSTEI together with the State Technical Library as well as the Patent Library will be situated.

As far as the problem of personnel is concerned, about 3% of information workers are today in the scientific and research basis and by 1970 their total should reach 4%. The new staff must be well trained and that is why we are preparing special training courses for information workers:

On the level of university and post-graduate studies

On the high-school and post high-school level

On the scientific level

Some of the training facilities have already been opened in Prague and in Bratislava. The principles of the training system are to be finished by autumn, to the extent that systematic training could begin in the school year 1968 – 1969. At the same time lectures for the users of information should be begun, which would serve to acquaint them with the possibilities of the information system and would teach them how to work with information.

In a short survey I have tried to acquaint you with all that is so promisingly added to my name as the title of my paper. I have no other choice than to confess that the better part of my paper is formed by the presidential address given at the 2nd National Conference of Czechoslovak Information System Workers by the director of our Centre.

The parts which deal with facts, proposals and actual plans cannot be adapted to the character of the audience and that is why I have informed you in short about the contents of the elaborated conception. I hope the style, contents and last but not least the reading itself were not so Continental and alien to you that you could not follow them with understanding.

PROGRESS IN SCIENTIFIC INFORMATION SERVICES AND THE ROLE OF THE WORKING SCIENTIST

H. W. THOMPSON, F.R.S.

St John's College, Oxford

Although I appreciated the invitation to give this paper my acceptance was something of a scandal, for I have little expert knowledge of newer methods of scientific documentation and information services, and as an old President of my College at Oxford used to say: 'If you have nothing to say, say nothing'. It is true, of course, that during the past four or five years in several official capacities I have become involved in discussions about scientific information services and have seen more closely some of the problems which now beset us. Also, like everyone else, I have experienced the difficulties of keeping up with current literature even within my own restricted field of research.

However, perhaps the main justification for my agreement to talk today is that in spite of carrying the customary overload of scientific administration, I still pretend and try to be a working scientist, and I have come to believe that unless working scientists themselves now get more interested in scientific information problems and play a bigger part in tackling them, the situation will become even more desperate.

If there is to be an unhindered spontaneous growth of scientific literature on the one hand, and an uncoordinated development of communication systems and methods for storage and retrieval on the other, we shall continue to see a rapid increase of entropy — that is to say of confusion. To prevent this, and even to unscramble the existing situation, some external influence must be brought to bear, and I suggest that at present the most obvious one to try is the enlistment of scientists themselves and the use of their particular expertise.

The position has been eloquently expressed in the report of the Weinberg committee, a panel of the President's Science Advisory Committee in the U.S.A. four years ago. "Transfer of information," they say, "is an inseparable part of research and development. All those concerned with research and development — individual scientists and engineers, industrial and academic research establishments, technical societies, Government agencies — must accept responsibility for the transfer of information in the same degree and spirit that they accept responsibility for research and development itself.

The later steps in the information transfer process, such as retrieval, are strongly affected by the attitudes and practices of the originators of scientific information. The working scientist must therefore share many of the burdens that have traditionally been carried out by the professional documentalist. The technical community generally must devote a larger share than hitherto, of its time and resources to a discriminatory management of the ever-increasing technical record. Doing less will lead to fragmented and ineffective science and technology."

It is now generally agreed that a nation's prosperity depends upon its science and industry. The health of the technical communication system must therefore be a concern of Government. Yet the highly critical power of scientists themselves in their technical literature, itself demands that Governments should work with scientists in all of this. It is my impression that the Governments of many of the most scientifically developed countries are now aware of this, and are prepared to play their part. It is less clear that scientists themselves have accepted their share of the responsibility. They must recognize this as a serious job, and not think that someone else should, or can, do something about it.

There are, of course, two parts to the problem: first, the growth in volume of scientific and technical literature, and secondly the need for better and quicker systems of filing, selective dissemination, and retrieval of documents and material for immediate use of later reference. Both these are international in character.

Lately, I have sometimes felt that in the frantic effort to solve the second part — the collection and dissemination of material — amid all the excitement surrounding the development of newer machine methods, not enough action is being taken about the first part. I wonder whether sufficient steps are being taken to control — without loss to science — any unnecessary proliferation or duplication of primary information. Perhaps some people feel that machine methods will soon cope with a vastly increased amount of primary information and even eliminate superfluity within it. If so, this seems to me a bad argument.

Today, much new scientific knowledge is passed on orally, but most of it through printed journals. In the years to come, it seems certain that changes will be made, perhaps using depositories for full length papers, or microforms for the original publication, that can be used by individuals or fed into machine systems. There may be a considerable increase in the amount of oral communication between scientists, perhaps even using new radio and telecommunication methods; but for some time at any rate the printed journal will be the major system, aided by authoritative reviews and periodicals giving a general picture of scientific development.

There is therefore good reason to prevent unnecessary publication in the journals. It is time that we discredited those whose motto is "publish or perish", and urged younger scientists not to enter the rat race for either personal or national prestige. Unfortunately, the advancement of the status of many younger scientists is now measured by some less enlightened authorities by the number and kilogram weight of their publications in their early years of research. It is regrettable, too, that some authorities demand the giving and publication of lectures at discussions and Symposia as a 'quid pro quo' for granting of travelling expenses. Preprints and private reports, even quickly published letters, have obvious value, but also have their disadvantages; sometimes they are merely ephemeral, and sometimes just scientifically wrong. Certainly it is very doubtful whether these documents should be subject to abstracting and storage services. Primary scientific information which is to be regarded as of sufficiently long-term value to be recorded should be subject to the well-tried and proved systems of critical refereeing, with insistence on brevity and clarity. Perhaps too we should encourage many more of the small specialized research conferences, the proceedings of which are not only not published, but which are forbidden to be published.

Now scientists themselves can control all these things if they wish to do so. They must also be taught and compelled in their publications to adopt agreed international language and methods which will assist those who have to perform the second task of storage and retrieval.

I now turn to this second part of the problem. During the past ten years, very great progress has been made in the use of machines for documentation and information services; and it is certain that in the coming years, bigger and better machines and computors will be developed having larger storage capacity and greater manipulative power. We hope too, that the difficult problems in the automatic translation of language may, to some extent at least, be overcome.

However, great advances in information services, using existing machines, need not wait for such improvements. Progress is not at present determined primarily by shortcomings in existing machines, which can perform the necessary operations of storage, retrieval, profile matching, type-setting, and so on. At present, what may be more important is to determine, in different fields of science, what key information to record and how this can be done most conveniently. This involves critical assessments by scientists themselves of the specifically important features, and the preparation of primary publications in a form which makes such key information clear. Certainly, more research is needed using machines, on a wide range of primary information, to find the best ways of collecting and supplying what the user requires.

Also, of course, machines are not always essential or even appropriate, and simpler methods are sometimes more convenient and adequate for users in particular fields of science.

In all of this exploratory development, there may be certain dangers which should be avoided. Science and technology can only flourish if each scientist interacts with his colleagues, and each branch of science interacts with other branches of science. There is a danger of fragmentation into many repetitious discoveries of new methods, sometimes even of systems which are conflicting or inconsistent with each other. The problem is not one for Government agencies alone, but for all scientists and technologists. As a result of many discussions in several countries during the past few years, a number of guide lines to future progress can now be laid down:

1 Scientists must acquire a bigger "current awareness" of the seriousness of the problem of scientific communication. They must co-operate in their primary publications by a proper choice of title, abbreviations and references, the use of key words recommended in official thesauri for different fields, and by the preparation of informative abstracts. Learned Societies and others responsible for scientific journals should insist on this, and authors must accept their responsibility.

2 Science students and post-graduate workers must be trained in the methods of handling information, how to use the literature systematically and efficiently, and about new machine methods. Education of this sort is not only essential if the new information systems are to be effective, but may also stimulate the flow of new ideas about these methods and help librarians. It may also — as a sort of "fall-out" — breed more professional documentalists.

3 The profession of information science must be recognized as worthy of high esteem. It must be made 'respectable'. It must be appreciated more widely that research in this field is an integral part of the whole structure of scientific research.

4 Scientists — working with the appropriate agencies — must experiment with different methods of information processing and control, types of indexing, the development of 'soft-ware' (programmes) for computors for obtaining information of different kinds; and while doing so, they must keep in mind the need for uniformity and integration, as far as possible, among the different disciplines.

5 Science information activities in Governments Institutions and organisations — although obviously essential and in some respects the driving force — should not submerge or dominate other non-governmental activities in which research scientists and technologists and scientific Societies can themselves take part.

6 There must be a coordination of all the efforts nationally, and mechanisms must be created for coordination or combining national activities on the international level.

In addition to, or as part of, these lines of approach, there should be more specialized information centres, and scientific Societies should again examine longer-term issues such as depositories of primary information. They should have one or more members of their staff assigned to the task of watching continuously all developments in the mechanisation of information services. Also, steps should be taken to ensure that different information systems and methods within a specific scientific field and the systems used in different disciplines, are compatible.

Now, we must be very glad that a lot has been done already during the past few years to follow these guide lines — both nationally and internationally. Agencies have been established in many of the larger countries, between some of which there is a strong co-operation – such as we see at this Symposium between the U.K. and Czechoslovakia. Also, on the international level, some of the leading inter-governmental and scientific organisations are becoming active in this field. Many of you are, of course, familiar with these different agencies, but perhaps I should mention some of them, in order to emphasise the large amount of current activity.

The U.S.A. has spent vast sums to provide information services in many scientific disciplines, such as chemistry, medicine, biology, physics, geology, agriculture, metallurgy and engineering, and has made plans to coordinate and stimulate this work by national committees at a high level.

The Chemical Abstracts Service has a huge programme covering all aspects of chemical information services using computors. It is hoped shortly to develop this service based upon the molecular structural characteristics of known compounds, and to relate these features to their physical and chemical properties. Another special part of the service is about to start on polymer chemistry, and it is expected that in due course special publications will be issued, compiled from the machine store.

MEDLARS, the Medical Literature Analysis and Retrieval Service of the U.S. National Library of Medicine started operation about three years ago, and from a store of medical data on tape, compiles the *Index Medicus* by computor type-setting, a subject-author index of articles, and lists of citations on special topics, as well as providing a facility for machine searching of the store.

For engineering, the U.S.A. has prepared a thesaurus of terms which form the basis of a mechanised bibliographical literature service, and a similar programme is in hand for metallurgy. The National Aeronautical and Space Administration (NASA) issues abstracts and indexes of American and foreign research reports, for which microforms are available, and from tape records is developing a selective dissemination service.

The Biological Abstracts organization in Philadelphia expects to have a mechanised abstracts service shortly; the American Institute of Physics is engaged, jointly with its British counterpart, in developing a large programme for physics involving the preparation of abstracts, and the mechanised production of primary journals. At the National Bureau of Standards, Washington, three agencies are concerned with the supply of scientific information: the Technical Information Exchange collects a library of technical literature about automatic data processing, which is available for all; the Clearing House for Federal Scientific and Technical Information sells reports on Federal-sponsored research and development projects; and thirdly, there is an agency for Standard Reference Data. This National Standard Reference Data System aims to produce and disseminate critically evaluated data on many aspects of physics and chemistry – nuclear data, atomic and molecular data, properties of materials in the solid state, data on thermodynamics and heat transfer, chemical kinetics, colloid and surface properties, and other such matters.

The Institute of Scientific Information scans over a thousand journals, records details and produces a Science Citation Index, which can be obtained in book or tape form. A current awareness service can be supplied from the tapes as a complement to Current Contents, the titles journal prepared by this organisation.

The Smithsonian Institute aims to go even further, and to provide up-to-date information about unpublished research in specialised fields, and keep track of such work in Governmental and non-Governmental organisations and in Universities.

Apart from all these agencies, there are, in the U.S.A., information services associated with many of the large establishments such as the National Institutes of Health, the Food and Drug Administration, the Department of Defence, and the Library of Congress.

Against this enormous background of activity in the U.S.A., contributions elsewhere sometimes seem small. However, much has been achieved here in the U.K., and for that a good deal of the credit in the recent past should go to OSTI, the Office for Scientific and Technical Information, by its stimulus and financial support.

In staging the Scientific Information Conference as long as 19 years ago, the Royal Society focused attention on the urgency of the problem, and since that time through its Scientific Information Committee has tried to exert an influence towards the provision of better services in the different scientific disciplines. It holds periodic meetings of the Editors of scientific societies and others concerned with publication matters and tries to take whatever action is necessary or appropriate for the common good. I have the feeling that in the U.K., – and indeed everywhere outside the U.S.A. – many scientific Societies may have been rather slow to visualize the considerable changes which may become necessary in primary publication, abstracting and dissemination of information – probably to a large extent through lack of money, but also because their members, the working scientists, have not so far been drawn sufficiently closely into the problems of mechanized systems. Nevertheless, a good deal has been done, and things are well on the move.

For many years past, *Physics Abstracts* have been prepared by the Institution of Electrical Engineers in association with the Institute of Physics and Physical Society. Recently a new publication, *Current Papers in Physics,* has been started and found useful. This group have now begun a joint study with the American Institute of Physics, of computor methods for abstracting in Physics and the establishment of a comprehensive information service. The National Electronics Research Council has been experimenting during recent years with a mechanized selective dissemination of information system, in which user profiles are matched to the information store. The responsibility for this organisation has now been taken over by the I.E.E., and the Institution of Electronic and Radio Engineers has been associated with it.

The Chemical Society, which performed a useful service by introducing its monthly classified list of *Current Chemical Papers* many years ago, is now experimenting with a research unit at Nottingham University, which in cooperation with American Chemical Abstracts Service is studying the effects of computor-based services upon the use of information by research chemists and biochemists. It is hoped that as this pilot scheme reveals the user needs more precisely, the service can be gradually improved.

The Institute of Chemical Engineers is compiling a thesaurus of terms, which will be compared with that recently prepared in the U.S.A., and the Royal Aeronautical Society is accumulating design data for engineers. The U.K. Atomic Energy Authority prepares from British literature an input to the *Nuclear Science Abstracts* published in the U.S.A., and similar material is supplied by the Electronic Materials Information Centre at Malvern to Oak Ridge.

For much recent progress in the U.K., however, we are indebted to OSTI, set up two years ago to promote activity in information problems and to coordinate the work of other agencies in this field. O.S.T.I. is helping to finance the Chemical Society's unit at Nottingham, and has sponsored a related study at Sheffield University where, in collaboration again with American Chemical Abstracts, techniques are being developed for the automatic detection of structural relations among compounds in a computor file, and their correlation with physical, chemical and biological properties. If this system can be established, the stored data may provide important information about chemical reactions and may even be used to suggest syntheses for unknown molecules. OSTI has also sponsored a centre for the collection of data on mass spectra at Aldermaston, from which a monthly Bulletin is now being issued, and it is hoped soon to use the store for identification, analysis and also for literature retrieval. OSTI is also supporting at Newcastle a study of the MEDLARS system, a compilation of intestinal absorption information at Sheffield University, a new centre for data on the science and technology of high temperature processes in Leeds University, and on thermochemical data at Imperial College It has also sponsored research on photographic copying and the preparation of micro forms (film or fiche); on the preparation of a thesaurus for the constructional engineering industry by the Royal Institution of Chartered Surveyors; and has established a number of industrial liaison centres at technical Colleges and Universities to stimulate local industries to make more use of existing knowledge.

As part of a wider educational programme, OSTI has helped to institute a post-graduate school of librarianship at Sheffield University, where a study is being made of the form and content of education and training required for work in libraries and information departments. It has also arranged courses at the National Lending Library, Boston Spa, with the object of teaching research students and academic staff of Universities as well as University Library staff, how to use the tools for current awareness, the abstracting and indexing journals, current reviews, technical language dictionaries, and related equipment. Such courses need now to be instituted by the Universities themselves.

Among general developments in the U.K., I should mention also the new course at the City University London, leading to a post-graduate degree in information science, and for which a good syllabus and scheme has been worked out. Conferences have been arranged, too, between scientific and professional librarians and information Scientists, such as that between the Institute of Biology and Aslib last December. More of these are desirable, and all these activities should further strengthen the membership and standing of the Institute of Information Scientists.

I have listed these many activities at some length — although the list is incomplete — as an indication of the considerable progress now being made. I shall not describe similar work which is being carried out in other European countries, in the U.S.S.R., and in Japan. Many of you are familiar with the large programme of VINITI in Moscow, and at this meeting you will hear about progress in Czechoslovakia.

I must, however, say a few words about some other international aspects. There are many international organisations concerned with information science, having different defined purposes, and sometimes — as far as I can tell — with overlapping interests. Some, like F.I.D., or I.F.I.P., are concerned mainly with general advances in techniques, terminology, the training of documentalists, or the translation of languages. Others, like I.A.E.A., F.A.O., W.H.O., or Euratom are more directly concerned with specific areas of science and technology.

For many years UNESCO has arranged working groups to study the form of primary publications, and to propose a code of good practice for them, to study the flow of scientific information, or to encourage the formation of associations of editors. Incidentally, on this last point, we should welcome the recent trends towards the formation of European federations of scientific societies or editors. Very recently such an association of biological editors has been established and there have been similar proposals for physics.

Recently, O.E.C.D. (the Organisation for Economic Cooperation and Development) has established a Science and Technology Policy Group which is at present trying to formulate its programme.

Perhaps the most interesting new international development is the surge of interest by the I.C.S.U. (International Council of Scientific Unions), since this body, through its Scientific Unions and National Members, may express the views and expertise of working scientists more directly than most others. During my own Presidency of the Council about two years ago, the Council decided to launch two new programmes. One special Committee, CODATA, is to survey the present world activities in the compilation of critically evaluated scientific data, to assess the needs and arrange for future compilation on an international basis. This work will obviously involve interplay with the National Standards Reference Data project at the National Bureau of Standards, and as a British contribution, OSTI has sponsored the first stages for setting up a Crystallographic data centre at Cambridge, in addition to that concerned with thermo-chemistry in London. Funds for this CODATA committee and its central administration have so far been committed by Governmental agencies in a few large countries. Here is a programme in which working scientists can make a direct contribution, either by sharing in the actual work of compilation, or by accepting rules which may have to be laid down so that estimated accuracy is clear in their primary publications.

The second new project of ICSU, which is to be carried out jointly with UNESCO, is the study during the next year or two of the feasibility of a world scientific information system. A committee to conduct this study is in process of being established.

I may also mention that ICSU proposes, during its next Assembly in Paris in June 1968, to hold a full day Symposium on Scientific Information and Communication, in the hope of enlisting a greater interest among its member scientists.

At the risk of being dull, I have given a factual account of recent progress. I think that it is sufficiently encouraging to provoke the question as to what more is needed to ensure rapid success. The facts are impressive enough to make the vision of the future methods of scientific communication, as described in an article last year by Vickery and Simpson, quite credible. In this, the scientist was able to make direct contact through a console with information stores in local centres or in central libraries; and if a means can be found for submitting his questions to the machine orally rather than through a typed programme, he would conduct a dialogue with stores of information, as if he were talking to another person who knew everything there was to know. Dialogues of this sort are indeed already beginning in the U.S.A. At the Massachussetts Institute of Technology and elsewhere, scientists are placing their questions to a machine store in the evening and return next morning to find the assembled information which they require.

The doors of the palace of Information Science are now open, inviting more scientists to walk in. I hope that they will.

SOME PROBLEMS ENTAILED WITH THE INVESTIGATION INTO THE INTEGRATED INFORMATION SYSTEM IN CZECHOSLOVAKIA

KAREL CIGLER

COSTEI, Prague

ABSTRACT

If we consider information activity as a social process — which it actually is — we see that it requires not only a common coordinated activity of the information system, but it must also observe the rules which govern every intentionally managed social activity, — taking into account the interests and requirements of information users.

Information is thus the basis of all social and economic processes and its utilization in the process of decision is defined only with regard to a certain aim. Obviously, the more numerous the groups of individuals which mutually co-operate, the more complex will be the interrelations originating thus and the more exacting will be the requirements in the information activity.

In order to make our suggestions on the suitability of certain information systems more exact the following preliminarily defined questions must be studied, viz:

Degree of integration of the information network and its services;

Extent of comprehensiveness of the information system and the questions pertinent to it, i.e. acquisition, storage, processing, availability and dissemination of information;

Links of the information system with other information systems of the world;

Stating of the hierarchy of information requirements, extent and order of meeting the demands of science and of managing and economic bodies;

Alertness, velocity, regularity, adaptability and extent of information;

Degree of mechanization and automation, as well as the influence of human factor on the activity.

There are principally three basic types of information systems, viz:
1 Decentralized information system with prevailingly horizontal information flows;

2 centralized information system with prevailingly vertical information flows;

3 combined information system consisting in the combination of horizontal and vertical information flows.

In the first, information exchange occurs on the basis of two mutually independent subjects, i.e. on the basis of exchange of two partners of the same level, none of which is superior or subordinate.

Such organisational structure of information activities with only horizontal information flows is nevertheless naturally limited and only individuals or, at the maximum, individual information centres, can cooperate in this way.

The complexity of demands for information activity, e.g. where the conditions for its operating are more complicated or where the aims to be attained are more exacting, it will be indispensable to develop more extensive co-operation, labour division, and to set up a completely different organizational structure of the information activity.

In branches with an extensive information activity the horizontal information flows cannot secure sufficient co-operation. On the other hand, if these information flows are completely excluded, all information activity must pass through a central unit, which results in slowing down the information flow. A central body requires an extensive administrative staff as otherwise some information must be left unprocessed and consequently unused. On the other hand, centralization of the information activities enables a concentration of means and a far better usage of mechanization and automation systems.

Nevertheless, it is necessary to consider carefully when centralization is profitable and what types of information centres to establish. With respect to their capacity such organization must be effected, which would secure optimum information loading of the selected system.

A combined information system compensates to some extent for the disadvantage of the two above information systems, maintaining at the same time their advantages. When stipulating fundamental principles for building up a new organization of the information system, it is necessary not only to evaluate carefully the suitability of the individual information systems, but in the first place to lay emphasis on the following qualitative indices which must comprise:

Preconditions for optimum control of the future organization.

Functional and intentional organizational structure aimed at maximum fulfilment of the main tasks.

Adequacy of the organization to the extent of the problems.

Adequacy to the developmental aims of the individual branches, disciplines or ministries.

Adequacy of the organization in relation to the comprehensiveness, integration and inner organization of the information system.

Adequacy of the organization in relation to theoretical knowledge of cybernetics, theory and organization of information.

Optimum harmony of mechanization and automation means in relation to the manual side of the organization.

Maximum materializing agreed standards and rationalization of principles and means in the future organization.

Adequacy of organization in relation to disciplinary and branch information networks.

PLANNING AND FINANCING SCIENTIFIC AND TECHNICAL INFORMATION IN CZECHOSLOVAKIA

VLADIMIR STEFANIK

Slovak Commission for Technology Bratislava

ABSTRACT

In Czechoslovakia the development of the national economy is secured by a system of economic plans, usually 5-year plans. This includes scientific information work, and a preliminary analysis of all research is prepared in advance, discussed in public discussions, and submitted to the State Commission for Technology. This framework is used:

Large scale information work in the form of separate informative stages or partial research problems that are planned long enough before other partial problems or stages of the research work itself.

Current awareness service to all partial problems, or stages, is planned within their framework.

The methods and forms of bonusing information pretreatment resulting from the above principles.

The research institutes responsible for co-ordination of large scale research problems (comprehensive tasks as they are called in our country) are also responsible for the co-ordination of information pretreatment necessary for these problems.

Financing of information services is included in the State development plan for science and technology. Some activities (about 25%) are expected to show a profit. Some costs are covered by the state:

(a) Costs of the independent information bodies belonging to the research and development basis (such as the Centre for Scientific, Technical and Economic Information in Prague, the Slovak Technical Library in Bratislava, and the largest disciplinary information centres) as well as the costs of information centres which form part of the state research institutes financed out of the state budget.

(b) The costs connected with information pretreatment of research and development problems of the state plan.

(c) Further costs of work of a more general character not included in the above mentioned categories are financed by grants. The grants are a supplementary form of financing and, therefore, centres financed directly from state budget do not receive them.

Industrial centres are financed as follows:

(a)   Information work for solved research and development problems is invoiced by the information centre to the responsible institute solving the problem at the level of amount spent (salaries, material, management etc.)

(b)   Information work ordered by the customer (individual reference lists, translations, multicopying etc.) is invoiced to the customer according to the real amount spent, with a possible reasonable profit.

(c)   The other activities (for instance the creation of primary and secondary holdings documentation, classification etc.) are financed by the organisation for which the centre works, or, as far as large-scale activity is concerned, are financed by state grants as mentioned above.

Internal planning of individual centres is not subject to one uniform method, but some standard principles have been evolved, based on:

(a)   the thematic (subject) plan of the centre's activity;

(b)   the plan of means and needs of the centre (including items concerning the building up primary and secondary holdings, translations, references and analyses, publishing etc.)

Some average time ratings based on my own observations and comparison with other socialist countries are as follows:

1	Average time for processing of one library unit (from acquisition to shelving)	35–40	minutes
2	Average time for library attendance (one unit)	15	minutes
3	The filing of one documentation card into the files	1	minute
4	Search of one documentation card in the files	3	minutes
5	Selection of articles for elaboration of documentation abstracts (average for one volume of periodicals)	30	minutes
6	Elaboration of a bibliographical entry from a document in mother tongue	15	minutes
7	Elaboration of a bibliographical entry from a document in a foreign language	20	minutes
8	Average time for the elaboration of a documentation abstract with annotation	40	minutes
8a	Elaboration of a documentation abstract with annotation from a document in mother tongue — officer 27½ minutes — typist 4½ minutes	32	minutes
8b	Elaboration of a documentation abstract with annotation from a document in current foreign language — officer 37½ minutes — typist 5½ minutes	43	minutes

8c	Elaboration of a documentation abstract with annotation from a document in another foreign language — officer 39½ minutes — typist 5½ minutes	45	minutes
9	Elaboration of an excerpt from a document in mother tongue	60–90	minutes
10	Elaboration of an excerpt from a document in a foreign language	120–180	minutes
11	Average time for a translation from a foreign language into mother tongue (1 typed page — 30 lines, 60 keys)	60	minutes
12	Average time for a translation from the mother tongue into a foreign language (1 typed page)	120	minutes
13	Professional editorial work in preparing materials for publication (1 typed page)	60	minutes
14	Technical editorial work in preparing materials for publication (1 typed page)	25	minutes
15	Average time for the elaboration of a bibliographical reference list	30	hours
16	Planned time for the elaboration of an information analysis	200–400	hours
17	A microfilm of the document (one shot)	1½	minutes
	a photocopy of the document (1 piece)	7	minutes
	a xerocopy of the document	3–10	minutes

THE SCIENTIFIC AND TECHNICAL INFORMATION NETWORK IN THE UNITED KINGDOM

EXISTING NETWORK

J. C. GRAY

Office for Scientific and Technical Information

The main components of the British information network are primary and secondary publications, general libraries, special libraries and information centres, data activities and special services for industry and agriculture. In addition, there are special services for information officers — training, research and technical advice.

PRIMARY PUBLICATIONS

These are traditionally a major contribution of the learned societies and professional associations, which also disseminate information through meetings, conferences etc. But a considerable proportion of the total output is in the hands of commercial publishers, which are also responsible for a large number of monographs, advanced textbooks, conference reports and special compilations. Government research stations and research associations are also extensive producers of non-periodical publications.

SECONDARY PUBLICATIONS

These are nearly 400 abstracting and indexing systems in Britain, but almost all of them are small and technological in character and they exist largely to provide specialised services to limited audiences more quickly than can be provided by the major systems. The bulk of them are organised by technological institutes, Government research stations, research associations and industrial firms and very often are prepared in research laboratories for use initially by the research staff and later, in printed form, by a wider readership.

Most of the major English-language disciplinary services are the responsibility of U.S. organisations, but a few are centred on Britain, notably "Science Abstracts", covering physics, electrotechnology and control; "Zoological Record" and the 13 abstracts journals produced by the Commonwealth Agricultural Bureaux and financed by Commonwealth governments. But some of the small systems are of high quality and complement larger systems in inter-disciplinary fields both at home and overseas; good examples of these are "Metallurgical Abstracts", "Mineralogical Abstracts", and "Index Kewensis".

GENERAL LIBRARIES

a) *Reference.* The principal scientific reference facilities are provided by the universities and colleges of technology; they are available mainly to staff and students, but most institutions make informal arrangements for other serious users. Public libraries in the larger towns provide technical, commercial and general reference facilities on an open basis and a few of them offer a good selection of scientific literature as well. Several big public libraries offer various kinds of service to readers and this practice is beginning to develop in universities and colleges as well. In London two major libraries are maintained as national institutions; the National Reference Library of Science and Invention, which forms part of the British Museum and incorporates the former Patent Office Library; and the Science Museum Library, administered by the Department of Education and Science, which has lending as well as reference functions. Scotland and Wales have their own national libraries, covering all subject fields.

b) *Lending.* Individual scientists borrow through their local libraries, whether academic, special or public, or through their learned societies. The traditional system of inter-library loans for all subject fields is based on informal local arrangements (bilateral and co-operative) and on a formal regional network, the apex of which is the National Central Library. This Library has a collection of its own, consisting mainly of literature not likely to be held elsewhere; but it meets most of its requests by consulting union catalogues of regional holdings and where necessary making speculative approaches to individual libraries. The slowness and uncertainty of this procedure led the Government in 1956 to set up a National Lending Library for Science and Technology in order to cater quickly and efficiently for the rapidly increasing demand by scientists and technologists. Administered by the Department of Education and Science, it seeks comprehensive coverage of serial literature and of certain categories of books, but confines itself to literature that records and interprets research or is otherwise necessary for serious study. It is run on industrial lines, and deals primarily with requests for specific items of literature, relying to a small extent on the Science Museum Library in dealing with requests for older literature. Recently it has started on an experimental basis to collect serials (but not books) in the social sciences. The Library's photocopying service is available to libraries in all countries, and use of it outside Britain has been growing rapidly in recent years. The Library is responsible for collecting and announcing British research and development reports and has recently begun to extend its collection of translations into English from Russian to all other languages. It is thus the national centre for reports and translations.

SPECIAL LIBRARIES AND INFORMATION CENTRES

The number of these varies according to the strictness of one's definition. The new "Aslib Directory" lists 3,000 sources of information in science and technology (excluding medicine) but only a small proportion of them have substantial resources and can offer a service in depth. Many of the important ones are in Government agencies or grant-aided bodies and the services of some are described in the Ministry of Technology's free booklet "Technical Services for Industry".

The organisations may be conveniently grouped under three sub-heads though some organisations range over two or even all three of them.

(a)　special libraries, in which the services offered are geared to, and generally result in, the loan of literature or the production of specialist bibliographies, and the staff are frequently professional librarians;

(b)　documentation centres, which process the literature in their fields, generally using subject specialists, and produce published guides to it (see sections on "secondary publications");

(c)　information centres, which scan and evaluate the literature in their fields, using subject specialists, and abstract specific information as a basis for dissemination services and answers to enquiries.

Many of the industrial organisations are mainly concerned with interpreting information for practical-minded users in industry. At the other extreme there are centres concerned mainly with the analysis of literature; but a number of organisations, e.g. research associations, cover both activities. Analysis of literature by specialists still active in narrow subject fields is little developed in Britain compared with U.S.A. and the Office for Scientific and Technical Information (OSTI) of the Department of Education and Science is supporting four experimental specialised information centres — in mass spectrometry, high temperature processes, bio-deterioration and intestinal absorption — in order to determine the potential role of such centres, expensive as they can be, in the information network of the future.

DATA ACTIVITIES

These fall into three main groups. Data on materials for industry are usually compiled by independent publishers, not always with critical evaluation; but some compilation is done by individual research, development or trade associations. Design data for engineers are sometimes published by research associations; but easily the biggest and most widely based is that run by professional institutions serving mechanical, aeronautical and chemical engineering, which is backed by a common Engineering Sciences Data Unit and supported by the Ministry of Technology.

Critical data for scientists, as in other technically advanced countries, are compiled by small teams in the universities and colleges and in the National Physical and Engineering Laboratories, often as part of international projects. However, OSTI in close consultation with the Royal Society and with other governments that have data programmes, is starting several experiments in the development of specialised data centres, each of which performs or is capable of performing an international function. The subjects covered by existing centres are crystallography (about to be extended to inter-atomic distances), mass spectrometry and the thermodynamic properties of certain gases. OSTI is also starting new data compilation projects in universities etc., and publishes a list of current data activities in Britain (see bibliography on page 30).

The Royal Society has set up a national committee to organise the British contribution to the ICSU CODATA programme. Both OSTI and the Ministry of Technology are represented on this committee.

SPECIAL SERVICES FOR INDUSTRY AND AGRICULTURE

Technical liaison services for industry, including information and advice, are provided by Government stations and by research, development and certain trade associations within their field of specialisation. A large number of Government stations and research associations fall within the responsibility of the Ministry of Technology and, to strengthen the links between its specialised services and industry, the Ministry has set up a network of nine regional offices which also administers a service for some 70 industrial liaison centres at universities and colleges. This Industrial Liaison Service is designed, mainly through personal contact, to strengthen contacts between industry, the universities and colleges and the specialised information services. Enquiries from small firms, which are not members of a research association or Aslib, tend increasingly to be routed through the Industrial Liaison Service.

The Ministry of Agriculture, through the National Agricultural Advisory Service, provides a range of specialised information and liaison services for agriculture, which is in many ways comparable with that of the Ministry of Technology.

SERVICES FOR INFORMATION SPECIALISTS

As in other countries the training of information specialists has until recently been based either "on the job" or in library schools. However, a number of specialised courses have been introduced in recent years and increasingly these are being planned as a result of careful surveys of need which are initiated and financed by OSTI. The range of existing courses includes full-time and part-time post-graduate courses and various short courses, notably those run by Aslib. First-degree courses and courses at technician level are among those planned for the future.

RESEARCH

Information research in Britain is also of fairly recent origin and most of it is supported by OSTI. Basic research is carried out mainly in universities and colleges, some but not all of it in libraries or in schools of librarianship or information science. Applied research and user studies are a primary concern of Aslib which is concentrating on studies of mechanised and information operations and which is building up through research, consultancy and other activities a modern service of technical advice for information officers. User and evaluation studies are also carried out by Government agencies and learned and professional institutions as part of experiments with new information services.

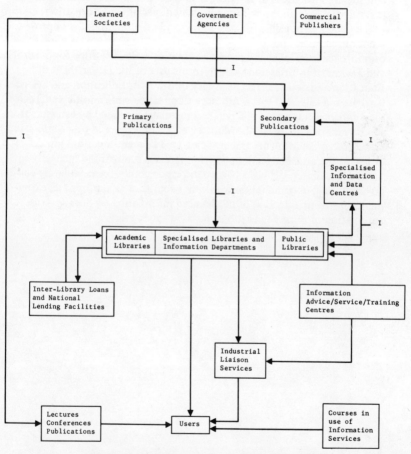

Tentative Diagram Showing Structure of Information Services

I indicates international links

NATIONAL RESPONSIBILITIES FOR INFORMATION ACTIVITIES

The Royal Society stimulates and co-ordinates the contribution of scientists to the development of information services and has set up a Committee on Scientific Information for this purpose.

Aslib is the national member organisation of the International Federation of Documentation and, with grant aid from OSTI, stimulates and co-ordinates the contribution of documentalists to the development of information services.

Government departments and agencies are responsible for developing information services for final users in their field of interest; in particular the Ministry of Technology has responsibility for ensuring that the very considerable resources of its research and development establishments are made available to industry through its own specialised information services.

The body responsible for stimulating and co-ordinating the improvement of scientific and technical information services as a whole and for promoting educational and research activities is OSTI (Office for Scientific and Technical Information), which forms part of the Department of Education and Science. The Secretary of State for Education and Science is advised in this field by an Advisory Committee on Scientific and Technical Information whose independent members are aided by assessors from the Royal Society, Aslib, the Ministry of Technology and other interested Government departments and agencies. OSTI's main functions are described in the attached leaflet and its progress is summarised quarterly in "OSTI Newsletter". It has a particular responsibility for stimulating and co-ordinating, in conjunction with other countries as appropriate, experiments in the introduction of mechanised information services and the automation of library operations, notably cataloguing.

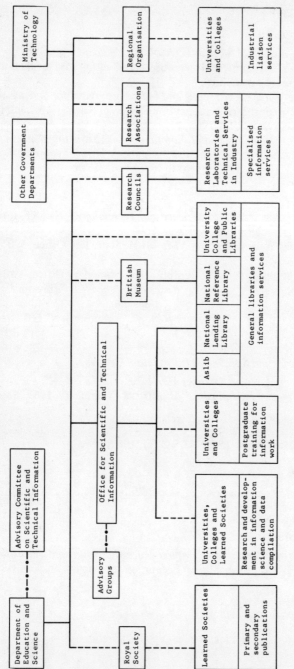

UNITED KINGDOM: Government Responsibility for Scientific and Technical Information

BIBLIOGRAPHY

Secondary Publications

"Abstracting Services in Science Technology, Medicine, Agriculture, Social Sciences, Humanities." International Federation for Documentation, 1965, 25 florins (Netherlands).

"Guide to the World's Abstracting and Indexing Services for Science and Technology." Report 102. National Foundation of Science Abstracting and Indexing Services, USA 1963, $5.

"Survey on the Organisation and Functioning of Abstracting Services in the Various Branches of Science and Technology." U.N. Economic & Social Council. UNESCO Series No E/3618, 1962. Free.

General Libraries

"National Lending Library for Science and Technology." NLLST, 1967, Free.

"Current Serials Received by the NLL." H.M. Stationery Office, 1965, £1. 7. 6d.

"NLL Translations Bulletin." (Monthly) H.M. Stationery Office, 4s.

"Index of Conference Proceedings Received by the NLL." (bi-annual), NLLST, free.

"British Research and Development Reports." (Monthly), NLLST, free at present.

Special Libraries and Specialised Information Centres

"Aslib Directory." Vol. I. October 1967.

"Technical Services for Industry." Ministry of Technology, 1967, Free.

Data Activities

"Critical Data in Britain 1966–67." OSTI, 1967, free.

Special Services for Industry

"Regional Offices and Industrial Liaison Centres." Ministry of Technology, 1967, free.

Educational Activities

"Proceedings of International Conference for Education and Scientific Information Work." International Federation for Documentation, 1967.

Research

"Scientific Research in British Universities and Colleges, 1966–67."
Volume I. Physical Sciences. H.M.S.O. £2. Volume II. Biological Sciences.
H.M.S.O. £2. Volume III. Social Sciences. H.M.S.O. £1. 12. 6d. (Each
volume has a section on information science).

OSTI

"Office for Scientific and Technical Information." OSTI, free.
OSTI Newsletter (Quarterly), OSTI. Free.

ORGANIZATION OF INFORMATION STOCK FOR EFFICIENT DATA COMPILATION

IVAN WIESENBERGER

Chair of Librarianship and Scientific Information, Charles University, Prague

ABSTRACT

I.   INTRODUCTION. (New model of information work in some information centres)

Our information network can be divided into three different stages, viz.:

1   information centres for various scientific, industrial and other disciplines of our national economy,
2   information centres for various branches of these disciplines,
3   fundamental ("primary") information departments of different national enterprizes, research institutes and other organizations.

In order to achieve the best knowledge of the different problems it is necessary to give to the users *not only the most relevant documents, but also the most appropriate scientific, technical and economic data.* For this, we can divide information stores into two separate parts: *the documentation part (store of documents) and the part containing different facts and experiments, and quantitative data concerning those facts and experiments.* This organization of information stock partly exists in our country already, especially in some information centres and departments of chemical, engineering, textile and food industries, and of chemical, geographical, geological, biological and other sciences.

II. CREATION OF FACTUAL DATA STORE. (Creation of information memory)

A factual data store — or information memory — has many advantages and only few drawbacks, as compared with other known memories (human or computer memories), namely:

1   its reliability of acceptance and of retrieval of the different data,
2   its durability and security of maintaining the data,
3   its great flexibility of changing obsolete and unnecessary data by replacing old data with new,
4   its great capacity (almost unlimited) of storing the most varying quantitative or qualitative data.

The questions for discussion in relation to users' needs may be:

1 What ideas, experiments, facts and data should be compiled in information centres, and filed in their stores?
2 What general designation should be chosen for such data, and in what way should these data be divided (critical, factual, reference, design, environmental, marketing data, etc.)?

III. MEDIA FOR FACTUAL DATA INPUT INTO THE INFORMATION STORE (MEMORY)

For effective data compilation it is necessary:
1 to collect data important for the activity of the centre itself, and
2 to systematically evaluate, classify and store the data for future retrieval and use.

For collecting the data *certain means and methods may be recommended to use*, as e.g:
 (i) observation forms (cards),
 (ii) questionnaires,
(iii) statistical lists
(iv) special kinds of entries,
 (v) excerpts,
(vi) cuttings, etc.

For the above evaluation, classification and storage of these data the following means and methods are mainly used:
1 producer files, and product files,
2 lists (directories) of competitor firms; lists (directories) of analogous institutes (organizations) and comparable products,
3 surveys, tables and diagrams,
4 "territorial paper files" and "product paper files",
5 "printed sheets", "printed cards" and "comparative cards",
6 peek-a-boo punched cards, edge punched cards, machine punched cards and magnetic tapes.

IV. MEDIA FOR DATA OUTPUT FROM THE INFORMATION STORE (MEMORY)

The aim of collecting, evaluating and storage of data is *to retrieve and disseminate them for the organizations which the information centres serve, and for the various needs of the users of these centres.* The main forms of dissemination used at our information centres are:
1 critical reviews and technical reports,
2 analytical studies,
3 other data collections, as e.g. surveys, tables and diagrams of scientific, technical and economic data.

The question arising here is: What forms are most suitable for dissemination and publication of data compilations?

V. CONCLUSION (Effectiveness of the New Model of Information Work)

In data compilation the following points should be mainly observed:
1 the principle of collecting the most current, complete and reliable data,

2 the principle of conciseness and clarity of the different forms of dissemination and publication,

3 the principle of differentiated method of dissemination according to various kinds of users,

4 the principle of co-operation with other information centres or departments and the principle of consultation with proper experts,

5 the principle of economy with regard to the cost of the information centres and to their relatively small personnel equipment,

6 the principle of using attractive and efficient means for the dissemination of data, either from the form or the content point of view,

7 the principle of using mechanical selection.

SYSTEMS ANALYSIS OF A UNIVERSITY LIBRARY

A. GRAHAM MACKENZIE

University of Lancaster

In presenting some account of the work being done at Lancaster on the systems analysis of a university library, I wish to make it quite clear at the beginning what I do *not* mean. We are not concerned with "scientific management" as defined in the recent book by Dougherty and Heinritz ([1]) — time and motion study, work measurement or work simplification, the redesign of forms and stationery, and all the other paraphernalia of low-level industrial or commercial management. These admittedly have their place, but only a minor one: it profits a library little if its procedures are all perfect, but all directed to the wrong ends.

We are *not* at this stage concerned with information retrieval on the grand scale for two reasons; first, we do not believe that it can ever be an economic possibility for individual large *general* libraries to do this — apart from anything else, the problem of input is immense; secondly, we do not believe that it would fulfil all of our needs: it is possible to set up a simplified model of a library as a store of discrete bits of information, each bit being identifiable by one or several index-entries or "addresses". The user is assumed to approach the store knowing what he wants, and the problem considered is how to deliver to him what he wants quickly, cheaply and with certainty. We might conceive as a future possibility the establishment of some vast central store of information, computer controlled, accessible by coded instructions passing over telephone lines from any part of the country or of the world, and delivering information by some teleprinter or television technique. In a limited field, such a study has been done; the Library of Congress report ([2]) recommends an expenditure of some $70 million for the complete transfer to computers of its catalogue and internal processes. This is excellent news for all concerned with information retrieval, "conventional" librarians and information officers alike, but to my mind it is putting the cart before the horse: it seems risky to spend sums of money of this order on work which does not go to the root of the problem of library use.

We agree that it may become economic to use the computer-controlled central store to deal with the accelerating increase in the mass of discrete items of information; but such a store would fulfil only part (and perhaps only a small part) of the functions of a library. Some people — perhaps as

many as half the total ([3]) — come to a library with a precise question:—
"What was the value of British imports of bananas in 1962?" But many
others come with a more general kind of question:— "Has anything been
written about banana imports which may throw light on my theory of
commodity trade?" They browse, they leaf quickly through a book to see
if it may help them, they follow up footnote references from one book to
another; they are interested in ideas or methods of presentation as well as
gobbets of information. There are strong indications that successful library
use at times depends on serendipity — or lucky discovery — rather than on
painstaking directed search. It is not clear that computer-controlled
information stores have any relevance to this more general type of library
use; in spite of Project MAC and Project INTREX ([4]) you cannot yet
readily browse in the memory of a computer. Much of the work on scientific documentation — indexing and retrieval, abstracting, the information
needs of scientists, the improvement of scientific journals, fundamental
work on the nature of communication through language, and on coding
and translation — seems to us to have in mind the simplified model of the
library as an information store to which precise questions are addressed.
But library policy should be based on what people actually need from
libraries. Comparatively little work has been done on this question; there
have been many attempts to find out what the library user actually uses,
but what he *uses* and what he *needs* are not necessarily the same
things ([5])–([7]). The consideration of actual needs may imply a complete
rethinking of the technical methods which are appropriate and economic.
On the face of it, indeed, the printed book which can be held in the hand
is well adapted to the needs of those who seek answers to questions which
are general and not precise. But it is not easy to transmit, without introducing delay or inconvenience, and the mass of printed knowledge is too
great, and growing too fast, to make it possible to assemble fully adequate
collections in (say) 60 university institutions in the United Kingdom. This
is the dilemma: and it is not answered by dealing only with the problem of
retrieving and transmitting precisely identified factual information.

The methods of use-study commonly employed have only a limited
relevance to the problem stated here: they may be able to state with some
accuracy what happens at present, and analyse the *scholar's* (rather than
"scientists", because we must consider the humanist as well) own evaluation
of what he believes he needs; but this is only a subjective judgement, and
will usually be made without a full knowledge of either the current situation or of potential developments. In information work it has often been
shown in the past that the supply of a facility very rapidly creates a
previously unthought-of demand, and the field has become so specialised
that few practising scholars are in a position to understand the present, let
alone forecast the future.

For these reasons, the University of Lancaster has in mind a long-term
programme for the investigation of the research worker in relation to his
sources of information and the interaction between them. This undoubt-

edly varies from subject to subject, and probably even from person to person. If a specific question cannot be answered immediately, is there a penalty in wasted time whilst the answer is obtained from another library? This will depend on the researcher's methods and whether he works on more than one project or aspect of a project at the same time. How does the penalty vary with the delay? Is there a cumulative effect so that the researcher becomes semi-frustrated and uses the library less frequently than he might? If he does, then is the problem of duplication of research severe and does the quality suffer? Is the quality of research reduced when browsing is restricted? Is there a limit to the amount of browsing which a man will do? Could the browsing be done at intervals in a regional library instead of in the local library? All these questions must be answered in a quantitative form. Once some generalisations such as these have been established, it would then be possible to derive some optimisations for such variables as the size, function and location of individual libraries.

For example, should an individual library purchase obscure books and journals if they are unlikely to be used frequently or by more than one man? Should there be a potential minimum usage for single books or should all the books on a topic be considered together? The results of such a study might be used to design a hierarchy of libraries, for which a balance would be struck between wasting money on purchasing "unnecessary" books and causing frequent duplication between libraries on the one hand, and wasting researchers' time and causing duplication of research on the other hand.

Such an investigation, however, still lies in the future; it is undoubtedly the most important section of the whole problem, but initially the University has restricted itself to a more immediate object, namely the study of a library system as it is. Little or nothing is known, in objective mathematical terms, of how existing libraries operate, and what has been published ([8])–([10]) is based on experience in the U.S.A., where budgets are much more lavish and operating conditions and users' needs are very different. In addition most of this work has been conceived as a necessary prelude to some form of partial or total mechanisation of the domestic economy of a library, rather than as a tool to aid management in decision-making – an example of this attitude is contained in the excellent pioneer study of the University of Illinois by Schultheiss ([11]), which analyses in extreme detail the technical processes involved in acquiring, cataloguing and issuing books, but ignores almost completely the purposes behind all these activities. This limited sense of systems analysis does not satisfy us; it needs to be done if we are eventually to mechanise our processes, but in a different and more restricted – even although a more detailed – way.

What *we* mean by systems analysis is much more far-reaching in its effects – in a few words, it is the use of scientific method to study the effects of managerial decisions in large-scale, complex situations. A librarian, like any other administrator, has to make many decisions in his routine work: generally at present these are the resultant of many conscious or unconscious forces — his previous training and experience, his innate prejudices, the internal politics of his organisation, even sometimes the state of his liver! Now the ecological system formed by a library and its readers is complex, delicately balanced and expensive; therefore decisions taken without full knowledge of the facts, and of the probable consequences of any given line of action, are likely to result not merely in trial and error, but in trial and disaster.

We need considerable justification for experimenting *in vivo* with a library system which has achieved a reasonable balance; the potential dangers are great. On the other hand, there is no such thing as the perfect library. How can we improve, then, without risking damage to the system? Obviously it is possible to tinker with small sections of a system — to re-design a form here, change a loan period or a rate of fine there — but the effects on some other segment of the library may be quite unexpected. Modern techniques of operational research are at our disposal, including the one essential tool of the mathematical model, which bears the same relationship to the object of study — in our case the library — as does an engineer's force diagram to the girders of a bridge he is designing.

How can we set about an operational research or systems analysis of a library? The normal procedure for such an investigation, let us say in a large industrial concern, is fourfold: first, to define the objectives of the company (perhaps maximum long-term profit within certain constraints such as the law of the land); second, to flow-chart all the processes which form the company, in whatever detail is required; third, to construct a mathematical model, using appropriate equations to describe each process or operation; and lastly, to use this model to optimise the company's operation so that the highest possible proportion of each of its stated objectives is attained.

Unfortunately, most O.R. studies are conducted in terms of profit-ability, where it is relatively simple to determine the objectives; but an academic library is a service organisation, and cannot look at its operations in this light. It is, of course, fairly easy to arrive at a first approximation of a library's purpose — the tentative definition which we have adopted is "to assist in the identification, provision and use of the document or piece of information which would best help a user in his study, teaching or research, at the optimal combination of cost and elapsed time", but unfortunately this raises many more questions than it solves. For example, bibliographical training of students will result in increased library use, and thus in higher operating costs in book purchases or inter-library loans; and yet this train-ing itself is also expensive in terms of salaries. If the sole criterion were financial, obviously we ought not to try to increase library use — but we should then be producing inferior students. Similarly, to invent an extreme example, we might interpret "at the optimal . . . elapsed time" in the definition of our objectives as meaning that we should maintain a helicopter and pilot to fly to the National Lending Library four times a day to collect loans for our scientists; the delay would thus be minimised, but at a cost which might prevent us from buying any books at all, and which in any case would far outweigh the value to the university of the readers' time which had been saved.

One solution to this problem which has been suggested is quite ingenious, and is in fact also being studied by a parallel investigation in the University of Durham: various aspects of a library's services (additional book purchase, improved inter-library loan service, improved reference service, SDI, free photocopying, extended opening hours, etc.) are assigned prices which, although nominal, bear some relationship to the true costs. Members of the university are then asked to imagine that they have at their disposal a certain fixed amount of money and to declare how they would wish to spend this on varying combinations of the proposed benefits. Although this is a standard technique in marketing operations, we see certain objections to its use in a library situation; in particular, that those asked are unlikely to be able to visualise in any detail the results, good or bad, which would come from these additional services if they were provided.

It is becoming clear to us that there are serious difficulties in formulating an academic library's objectives in relation to its research readers, and hence in optimising its performance, unless we can find out more about the function and performance of the research worker himself, as outlined earlier in this paper. We are therefore trying to proceed to the second and third stages of the analysis, by flow-charting and by constructing a simplified model which can be made more sophisticated as our knowledge grows.

A few of the equations for the construction of this dynamically balanced model have already been formulated, and a start has been made on quantifying some of the variables which will have to be built into it. It is our expectation that when the model is complete, even in its simplified state, we shall be able to inject into it any number of differing managerial decisions and investigate how these will affect the system with the passage of time. (It would, of course, be equally possible to inject existing decisions to see whether they are likely in the long run to have the intended effect — the aim of this type of model is to simulate either backwards from the optimal end-state or forwards from any set of decisions, provided that the model itself and its associated computer programmes are sufficiently sophisticated and initially represent all the required inputs and outputs.) An example of the basic structure of one part of the model is given in the appendix, although since the project is still in its early stages this must be regarded as highly provisional and unsophisticated — for example we have not built in the space requirements for storage, staff and readers, on the financial implications of different grades of workers.

Simultaneously with the investigation of the technical processes of a theoretical model of a library we are looking at the actual provision of textbooks for students at Lancaster. We are perhaps in an unusually favourable position to do this, since there is a collection of over 2,000 volumes representing material which departments consider to be essential reading for undergraduates' lectures, essays and seminars. This collection is stored on closed-access shelving, and books are issued for periods of up to four hours or overnight; we can therefore easily analyse the use made of it (as a library which merely has a "reference" collection of this type of material cannot do), and, equally important, we can study with complete accuracy what we call the frustration factor – the proportion of enquirers who do not get the book they want at the first attempt. To our surprise, during two weeks just before an examination period, this proportion averaged only 11%, indicating that the system was working reasonably well. We have plans to correlate the use of this short-loan collection with a record of lecturers' recommendations to students, and hope eventually to be able to predict with some accuracy the number of copies of a title which would guarantee a given availability rate in any particular set of circumstances; and it should also be possible to extend this theory to the provision of all books required by undergraduates, although data collection is much more difficult in an open-access collection. This type of experiment demonstrates that quantification which is originally undertaken for the sake of model-building has an immediate relevance to the routine operation of a real library – our subjective impression had been that the average frustration factor was about twice as great as the figures demonstrate.

This exercise in data collection also suggests a possible index of a library's performance, and hence a quantifiable set of objectives, which might be difficult to specify in any other way. If we assume a constraint imposed on the system by the maximum financial support available to the library, and specify levels of availability of printed materials for different classes of users, it should be reasonably easy to predict from the model what the results are likely to be in terms of the system as a whole, and by managerial decision to adjust frustration factors to optimal levels. We do not believe that this is the complete answer to the problem of defining objectives, but it is certainly an improvement on the hit-and-miss method of reaching decisions which is currently followed.

A further valuable result of model-building is that it will inevitably draw attention to areas where further research is needed, and thus aid us in formulating more precisely the major investigation into the total dynamic ecological balance between information and its users; we realise that we are only at the beginning of a project which may take many years, and that it may not be possible to achieve the results which I have optimistically foreshadowed in this paper. Nevertheless, we believe that the exercise is well worth while; the mere process of analysing in detail what we do from day to day must bring a deeper understanding of our eventual objectives, and this in itself will help to smooth the channels through which information flows.

ACKNOWLEDGEMENTS:

The work of model building is being financed by a grant from the Office for Scientific and Technical Information; I wish to record my

gratitude to that body, and to Ian Woodburn and M. K. Buckland
(Research Fellow and Assistant Librarian (Research) respectively), who
have contributed many useful ideas to this paper.

REFERENCES

1   DOUGHERTY, R.M. and HEINRITZ, F.J. *Scientific management of library operations.* New York, Scarecrow Press. 1966.
2   Automation and the Library of Congress: a survey sponsored by the Council on Library Resources. Library of Congress, 1963.
3   HANSON C.W. 'Research on user's needs: where is it getting us?' *Aslib Proceedings, 16,* ii, 1964, 64–78.
4   OVERHAGE, C.F.J. and HARMAN, R.J. (eds.). INTREX: report of a planning conference on information transfer experiments. Cambridge, M.I.T. Press. 1965.
5   Information methods of research workers in the social sciences: proceedings of a conference . . . edited by J.M. Harvey. Library Association, 1961.
6   Science, government and information: Report of the President's Science Advisory Committee, U.S.G.P.O., 1963.
7   MENZEL, H. 'The information needs of current scientific research.' *Library quarterly, 34,* i, 1964, 4–9.
8   BECKER, J. 'System Analysis – prelude to library data processing,' *ALA Bulletin,* April 1965, 293–296.
9   LEIMKUHLER, F.F. *Operations Research in the Purdue Libraries in Automation in the library, when where and how.* Purdue University, 1965, 82–89.
10 LEIMKUHLER, F.F.'Systems analysis in university libraries.' *College and Research Libraries, 27,* i, 1966, 13–18.
11 SCHULTHEISS, L.A., CULBERTSON, D.S. and HEILIGER, A.M. *Advanced data processing in the university library.* New York, Scarecrow Press. 1962.

D

APPENDIX

Simple model of some consecutive technical processes with a built-in optional decision rule

The system is represented as a number of stages through which material passes for processing. We assume that the time scale is divided up into intervals of time (e.g. hour or week) referred to as slots during which the flows of work and labour are constant.

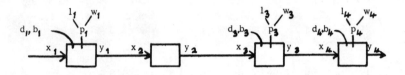

x = input rate (items per slot)
l = labour allocated (manhours per slot)
w = processing rate (items per manhour)
p = processing capacity (items per slot)
b = backlog at end of slot
d = delay to next item assuming serial processing (slots)
y = output rate (items per slot)

Consider the system in time slot (t).
Decision rule allocates just enough labour to clear backlog in one time slot.

1 *Ordering*

If decision rule then $l_1(t) = \dfrac{b_1(t-1) + x_1(t)}{w_1(t)}$; otherwise $l_1(t)$ given.

$p_1(t) = l_1(t)\, w_1(t)$

$y_1(t) = p_1(t)$ if $b_1(t-1) + x_1(t) \geqslant p_1(t)$

$y_1(t) = b_1(t-1) + x_1(t)$ otherwise.

[Because input rate might be less than processing capacity.]

$b_1(t) = b_1(t-1) + x_1(t) - y_1(t)$

$d_1(t) = b_1(t) / p_1(t)$

2 *Bookseller*
Assume distribution of supply times.
$f(i)$ = fraction of books supplied during the i th slot since order despatched.

$$x_2(t) = y_1(t)$$

$$y_2(t) = \sum_{i=0}^{i=\infty} f(i)\, x_2(t-i)$$

3 *Accessioning*

x_{31} input rate of purchased material (items per slot)

x_{32} input rate of donated material (items per slot)

$$x_{31}(t) = y_2(t)$$

$$x_3(t) = x_{31}(t) + x_{32}(t)$$

If decision rule then $l_3(t) = \dfrac{b_3(t-1) + x_3(t)}{w_3(t)}$;

otherwise $l_3(t)$ given.

$$p_3(t) = l_3(t)\, w_3(t)$$

$$y_3(t) = p_3(t) \text{ if } b_3(t-1) + x_3(t) \geqslant p(t)$$
$$y_3(t) = b_3(t-1) + x_3(t) \text{ otherwise.}$$

$$b_3(t) = b_3(t-1) + x_3(t) - y_3(t)$$

$$d_3(t) = b_3(t) / p_3(t)$$

4 *Cataloguing*

$$x_4(t) = y_3(t)$$

If decision rule then $l_4(t) = \dfrac{b_4(t-1) + x_4(t)}{w_4(t)}$

otherwise $l_4(t)$ given.

$$p_4(t) = l_4(t)\, w_4(t)$$

$$y_4(t) = p_4(t) \text{ if } b_4(t-1) + x_4(t) \geqslant p_4(t)$$
$$y_4(t) = b_4(t-1) + x_4(t) \text{ otherwise.}$$

$$b_4(t) = b_4(t-1) + x_4(t) - y_4(t)$$

$$d_4(t) = b_4(t) / p_4(t)$$

ADVANTAGES OF A LOCALLY INTEGRATED PUBLIC LIBRARY SYSTEM

WM. R. MAIDMENT

Camden Public Library, London

My choice of title must not be taken to imply any opposition to co-operation between libraries. No librarian can possibly ignore the fact that the time of skilled cataloguers and classifiers is largely employed on tasks which are duplicated elsewhere. In the U.K., there are some 470 separate public library systems and there can be little doubt that many current British publications are added to every one of those libraries. Some of them already use a form of co-operative cataloguing, usually based on the *British National Bibliography,* but there must still be several hundred entirely independent cataloguing departments with cataloguers and classifiers dealing with the same titles at approximately the same time.

This is not, of course, a new situation. The problem has existed for years and there have been many attempts to solve it. Some would claim that it has, in fact, been solved already by the existence of national bibliographies giving class numbers and, both in this country and in the United States, printed catalogue cards are available. The limited use made of this material is due to three main factors: firstly, there is always a delay in supplying the nationally produced catalogue information to the local library; secondly, the material produced has to be incorporated into an existing catalogue and the form of entry may not be readily compatible; thirdly, it has been necessary to retain a local cataloguing department to deal with foreign books and with older material not currently catalogued by the national organisation.

It may be that some or all of these difficulties in co-operation will be eliminated by the machine readable catalogue. If this is so, I will be one of the first to make use of the new service and to re-direct the professional staff time now being used in work duplicated elsewhere. Although this will be a welcome development I am unable to avoid pointing out that I have to use the future tense. This is a hope for the future and, moreover, one which will at best achieve a small, though useful, saving in professional time.

The basic advantages of the locally integrated system are two. Firstly, it is available now for anyone who cares to introduce it and, secondly, although it gives no economy in professional staff, it offers a large saving in clerical work. My own introduction of such a system has not been in a logical, planned order but has followed from a rather hasty production of a computerised catalogue to meet a new situation. From this first step towards automation I have realised that information already stored in the computer for the catalogue could also be used for stock control, for book charging and for a number of other "housekeeping" purposes.

Let me first describe what has already been done. On 1st April 1965 the London Borough of Camden was formed by amalgamating three smaller boroughs, Hampstead, Holborn and St. Pancras. The catalogues of the three existing libraries were not compatible with each other and it was obvious that a completely new catalogue would have to commence from the date of incorporation of the new borough. My main problem was that each of the smaller areas had maintained union catalogues. Each of the five libraries in Hampstead had a public catalogue showing all the books in all five libraries. The position was the same in the former Holborn and St. Pancras areas. To abandon union catalogues and provide each library with a local record confined to its own stock would clearly be a reduction in the standard of service, scarcely an auspicious way to begin in the new borough. To provide union catalogues in card form for every service point by conventional means would require an enormous amount of clerical work which I was anxious to reduce. I accepted that the main catalogue entry had to be prepared whatever the form of the local records. Once this entry was ready, the steps needed to provide union catalogues on cards would be as follows:—

1 The main entry would have to be reproduced for each library and, allowing for author, subject and other necessary entries, I assumed three cards would be needed for each title. During the first year we added some 15,000 titles and this means about 45,000 cards would be produced for every service point.

2 The cards would need to be sorted for despatch to the various libraries, each branch librarian receiving very nearly 1,000 cards every week for incorporation in his main catalogue.

3 Each branch librarian would need to find staff time for filing these cards, for removing cards representing withdrawn books and for amending the existing cards when locations were altered.

In addition to the enormous amount of filing and sorting of cards required by this system it also had the disadvantage that even the smallest branch library would have to find space for the necessary cabinets for a very large catalogue.

Compare all this with what has actually happened. The main entry for each book is transferred to two 80-column punched cards. These are read into the computer and the information is stored on magnetic tape. Every fortnight an author list of additions is printed out and the lists are cumulative. This means that every fortnight the Central and branch libraries receive a new printed list and the only task the staff have to perform is to throw away the superseded list. Every four months a complete printed catalogue, arranged by class number and provided with author and subject indexes, is produced. Again, there are no important clerical routines and the librarians merely throw away the old catalogue and substitute the new one.

A specimen page of the main catalogue print-out is before you and I am sure you will have noticed that it is by no means a piece of beautiful printing. It does, however, give the essential facts of what books we have and also indicates where they are, the letters in the right hand column representing the various libraries. The rather wide spaces occurring in some entries are necessary because we are using a fixed field system, allocating a number of columns to class number, to author, title, and so on. The catalogue has now been running in its present form for just over 2 years. There have been minor modifications to the program to enable us to provide a title list for fiction and a separate catalogue for children's books but the basic scheme is unchanged. It has served us well; there have been no major snags and we are now ready to move to the next stage.

From October this year I propose to abandon the fixed field system. The intention is that the cataloguers will work direct to a tape typewriter, thus cutting out the intermediate stage of card punching. By introducing an "end of field" symbol we shall achieve much greater flexibility since as much space as is needed can be used for class number, author or title provided only that the "end of field" symbol is typed before the next group. This will close up the type on the printed catalogue and improve both appearance and ease of use. The number of fields is being greatly increased so that the whole of our stock control will be done by computer, the first entry being made when a book is ordered and, from that point onwards, all the clerical routines will be computerised. This is not a mere hope for the future but a practical plan already well advanced, most of the system analysis is finished and part of the program is already written.

I realise that, if regionally or nationally produced tapes are available at some time in the future, I may have to face the problem of integrating the material with my own program. To some extent this problem will exist in any event for all librarians, since it is most unlikely that all their intake of books, British, foreign and replacements of older works, will be provided for entirely outside their own library. Some problems of integration are bound to arise for everyone. It may be that I am adding to them but, in the meantime. I am gaining useful experience of a fully computerised stock control system and, because of the very considerable savings in staff time, my programming and other overheads will have been recovered within months rather than years. Even if I have to change the whole of my present practice in order to co-ordinate with a national or international scheme at some time in the future I am positive that this is worthwhile even as an interim scheme. Some of the problems of integration may prove easier than we expect; I am satisfied, for instance, that all my existing material, as shown on the specimen pages you have, can be incorporated in the new, more flexible system without difficulty. We shall run all our existing tapes on a simple program to insert "end of field" symbols at the end of each fixed field.

I ought to make it clear that when we began the computer catalogue it was not possible to use the Borough Council's own computer. A new computer was on order for Camden but, initially, the programming staff were clearly going to be fully occupied with accountancy and other problems. The library work was therefore put out on a contract basis to the computer manufacturers, thus ensuring that the program, magnetic tape store and so on could be transferred to our own computer later. It will be at the time of transfer that we shall adopt the enlarged program already described.

The important point that arises here is that I am satisfied that our computer work has proved worthwhile on a purely economic assessment, even though we have had to contract the work outside our own organisation. When we transfer the task to our own computer we should find it very much cheaper still. I want to emphasise this point, because I do not think that public libraries or university libraries which do not have access to a computer owned by their own organisation need feel that they are excluded from any form of mechanisation. Rented time on someone else's computer is not necessarily prohibitive in cost and it is likely to become cheaper in the future. Smaller libraries might well want to reduce their capital costs by group arrangements for a shared program but this is not difficult to achieve. It is probable that the financial advantages of a computer-printed catalogue depend upon the number of copies of the catalogue that have to be maintained rather than on the total number of entries in each catalogue.

The advantages of using the book information for other purposes, once it is recorded in machine readable form, almost certainly apply to every library. My own extension of use will, as I have said, involve first a complete stock control and book ordering system. The next step will be to use the stored book information as the basis of a book charging system. Programming for this is already in hand and the complete system should be functioning in at least one of my libraries before the end of the year. The programming for a book charging system is not a very complex task and any librarian who contemplates such a system will find that his most difficult problem is to choose the equipment to be used for collecting data at the library counters.

There are already various systems available and several have had field trials. The simplest but not the best way is to use a tape typewriter and type the information about book issues and returns at the time of each transaction. If the loan records are done by using book numbers and reader numbers the possibilities of error by transposing figures or by miscopying seem to me to be unacceptably high for busy libraries. Various ways of automating the procedures are available and these generally use some form of punched card or ticket for each book and each reader. At the issue counter the reader's card is inserted in a scanner and book-cards for each book are read at the same time. At the return counter only the book card needs to be recorded to cancel the transaction.

Where a single library unit is involved or where the departmental libraries form a compact group there may be advantages in linking the data collectors to the computer in an "on-line" system. In a university library, where up-to-the-minute locations of books may be important, the "on-line" system may well be justified. For most public library systems it is sufficient to produce punched paper tape at the data collectors and read this onto the computer at set intervals, daily or even weekly.

Provided the book numbers for issue purposes are linked with the stored catalogue information it now becomes possible to eliminate all the clerical routines of book issue and return, of overdue notices and book reservations completely. The computer will handle all the records of a book from the time it is first ordered for the library until it is withdrawn or lost, if that should be its fate. My own progress towards this complete system is, as you will have gathered, only about half way but already the benefits are substantial. Financial gains have already been mentioned but I also value highly the increased accuracy of the system and the fact that our records are up-to-date. There are never arrears of filing, withdrawals or amendments of records accumulating until someone has time to attend to them. Amendments to the computer catalogues, by the way, are very simply arranged; an entry is identified by page number and entry number on the page and a simple coding adds or deletes locations as required.

I will, of course, answer any questions on the practical aspect of this integrated computer system but my task is primarily to discuss the general policy questions involved. It is odd that librarians have apparently approached the possibilities of computers in an entirely different way from workers in other fields. In most professions progress has been made by tackling first the relatively simple day-to-day clerical work and, later, looking at more complex problems. Accountants, for instance, first used the computer for book-keeping records, calculations of salaries and wages and similar tasks. Perhaps they were compelled to do this because the early computers were not capable of much more than this but, whatever the reason, the accountants had acquired a good deal of experience in using computers before they considered their use for more complex questions of economic research, market analysis and so on. When librarians began to consider computers comparatively advanced versions were available and the profession, it seems to me, has tried (perhaps I should say "is trying") to run before it has learnt to walk. Very complex problems of information retrieval and subject analysis have been considered before we have had much experience of using computers on the relatively simple jobs of clerical routines. Even now, when the profession is more aware of the possibilities of cataloguing and bibliographical work by computer, many librarians are thinking first of national or even international schemes of co-operation before they have attempted to solve the problems in their own libraries.

It may be that this global approach will one day prove to have been right; the skills and benefits may spread gradually downwards from international co-operation to the individual library but such a development would be almost without precedent. In the past we have built from the bottom upwards. Techniques developed locally have been shared amongst small groups and gradually increased their significance and range. It is just as likely that co-operative cataloguing will be achieved by one library marking the entries in the printed catalogues of larger libraries and having suitable magnetic tapes prepared on a selective basis. Even if regional, national or international schemes do come first their products will be much better received by librarians who have had some experience of automation in their local processing. Such experience will be of great value in dealing with the complexities of integrating the externally produced catalogue entries with the locally produced stock record. Even the apparently simple task of marrying the entry with the physical book will require very careful organisation in large libraries.

The advantages of the local system that I have so far mentioned are all based on direct experience or on firm estimates of extensions of that experience. There are more exciting prospects that I have not yet explored. I am sure we shall not be content to go on identifying our books and our readers by numbers which are no more than serial digits. Through the notations of our classification systems we are all familiar with the use of significant numbers and I do not think it should be beyond our skill to devise numbers for our books to indicate at least the broad subject grouping, the academic level, perhaps the date and to combine such significant digits with a serial section to identify a specific volume. Reader numbers, too, can combine their identifying function with significant digits indicating age, sex, educational level and so on. Only by these means shall we be able to use the analysing capabilities of the computer to the full advantage.

Every public library accumulates records of books and readers which are used almost solely for the restricted purpose of the day to day business of recording the issue and return of loans. A wealth of sociological and educational information is incidentally in our hands and, for want of a simple system of analysis, we largely ignore it. We ought to be able to provide the sociologist and the educationalist with facts about reading habits and their relationships with numerous factors in the environment. With the computer we can certainly do this. We ought also to utilise facts about book use in our own policy-making to a far greater extent than we have done in the past or, indeed, have been able to do. I envisage, for example, analysing the registered readers by address, to find out the effective "catchment" area of each library. The result of this research might well be of value in deciding the ideal sites for branch libraries. Analysis of book use would yield facts to aid book selection, transfers to reserve stock and even guidance on shelf arrangement. The impact of ascertained facts on many aspects of library policy and administration could be considerable.

Call No.	Author	Title / Publication	Code
650.018	ANSOFF ,H. IGOR	CORPORATE STRATEGY MCGRAW HILL 1965 241P.	ABC
650.03	ZAVADA ,DUSAN	ENGLISH CZECH COMMERCIAL DICTIONARY ORBIS 1955 519P.	B
650.07	FAIRHEAD ,J N , AND OTHERS	EXERCISES IN BUSINESS DECISIONS A MANUAL FOR MANAGEMENT EDUCATION	B
650.072	RIGBY ,PAUL H	CONCEPTUAL FOUNDATIONS OF BUSINESS RESEARCH WILEY 1965 215P.	ABCM
650.083	CROXTON ,FREDERICK E ,AND COWDEN	PRACTICAL BUSINESS STATISTICS 3RD ED PRENTICE HALL 1960 701P.	B
650.083	FREUND ,JOHN E ,AND WILLIAMS	MODERN BUSINESS STATISTICS PITMAN 1959 REPR. 1965 539P.	B
650.114	HEAD ,F D	FORMATION AND MANAGEMENT OF A PRIVATE COMPANY 5TH ED. BY MARGARET BOOTH 1962	A
650.12	FINANCIAL EXECUTIVES RESEARCH FOUNDATION	MERGERS AND ACQUISITIONS PLANNING AND ACTION ROUTLEDGE & K PAUL 1965 229P	AB
650.15	DEAN ,JOEL	MANAGERIAL ECONOMICS PRENTICE-HALL 1951 621P.	L
650.15	KOHLER ,ERIC L	ACCOUNTING FOR MANAGEMENT PRENTICE-HALL 1965 275P.	ABE
650.15	SLOUGH COLLEGE	CASE STUDIES AND SURVEYS BY THE MANAGEMENT ACCOUNTING RESEARCH UNIT 1965	AB
650.152	ALFRED ,A M ,AND EVANS	APPRAISAL OF INVESTMENT PROJECTS BY DISCOUNTED CASH FLOW CHAPMAN & HALL 1965 500P.	B
650.152	MASSE ,PIERRE	OPTIMAL INVESTMENT DECISIONS PRENTICE HALL 1962	A
650.152	WILLIAMS ,BRUCE R ,AND SCOTT	INVESTMENT PROPOSALS AND DECISIONS ALLEN & U; 1965 100P.	AB
650.154	COURT ,M P	BUDGETARY CONTROL SWEET & MAXWELL 1951 REPR. 1961 202P.	H
650.2	DIXON ,A A	NOTES ON COSTING PITMAN 1965 77P.	B
650.2	BRECH ,E F L	ORGANIZATION THE FRAMEWORK OF MANAGEMENT 2ND ED. LONGMANS 1965 561P.	ABCDEFHILM
650.22	LITTERER ,JOSEPH A	ANALYSIS OF ORGANIZATIONS WILEY 1965 471P.	AB
650.261	LAL ,R B	ART OF WORKING ASIA 1962 188P.	AB
	LINDORFF ,DAVID -	THEORY OF SAMPLED-DATA CONTROL SYSTEMS WILEY 1965 305P.	B
650.3	BEACH ,DALE S	PERSONNEL THE MANAGEMENT OF PEOPLE AT WORK COLLIER-MACMILLAN 1965 784P.	ABO
650.3	CRICHTON ,ANNE	PERSONNEL MANAGEMENT AND WORKING GROUPS INST; OF PERSONNEL MANAGEMENT 1962	B
650.3	DALE ,ERNEST ,AND URWICK	STAFF IN ORGANIZATION MCGRAW HILL 1960 241P.	B
650.3	PIGORS ,PAUL ,AND MYERS	PERSONNEL ADMINISTRATION 5TH ED. MCGRAW-HILL 1965 857P.	AB
650.31	URIS ,AVREN	EXECUTIVE JOB MARKET MCGRAW HILL 1965 276P.	B
650.31	AVENT ,CATHERINE ,AND FRIED	STARTING WORK PARRISH 1965, 139P.	A
650.311	GUION ,ROBERT M	PERSONNEL TESTING MCGRAW-HILL 1965 585P.	AB
650.311	LOMAX ,E S	INTRODUCTORY GUIDE TO SYSTEMATIC PERSONNEL SELECTION E.S. LOMAX LTD. 1964	B
650.311	LOPEZ ,FELIX M	PERSONNEL INTERVIEWING THEORY AND PRACTICE MCGRAW HILL 1965 326P.	A
650.3124	SARTAIN ,AARON QUINN ,AND BAKER	SUPERVISOR AND HIS JOB MCGRAW HILL 1965 464P.	B
650.4	SCHUH ,J F	PRINCIPLES OF AUTOMATION WHAT A ROBOT CAN AND CANNOT DO PHILIPS 1965 380P.	A

When we turn from our own preoccupations to the world around us I have some doubts about how far we shall be able to use the information we acquire. It will probably be technically possible in the future to tell educationalists a good deal about the effect of particular kinds of teaching on subsequent reading habits. Conversely it may be possible to discover whether reading particular kinds of books has any special effect on character or development. Are people influenced by reading? Does reading, apart from the immediate pleasure or gain, have any permanent effect on opinions, outlooks and even behaviour? We know very little about these matters but the possibility of finding out is opening up before us. This, I think, is an important aspect of computer use and one that must be kept in mind in deciding whether or not to change a system. The computer enables us to do things that could not be done in any other way. I am sure that most libraries would find sufficient justification for computerisation in the financial saving, in increased accuracy and in up-to-date records but I do not think these factors, important as they are, should be decisive. New ways of analysing our work, new approaches to our problems enabling decisions based on facts rather than on impressions or on guesses: these are the decisive factors.

NATIONAL AND INTERNATIONAL CO-OPERATION IN LIBRARY AUTOMATION

L. J. VAN DER WOLK

Delft Technological University Library, Holland

We have to bear in mind that at a certain moment not so very far ahead the automation of academic and scientific libraries will be a fact. Some people predict that already in 1976 we will have reached that point. Many things will have to be done before that important date so that it is necessary that we join forces. But is is not only for that reason that we have to co-operate.

I. CO-OPERATION IN THE DEVELOPMENT PERIOD

First of all we will have to co-operate during the development period of our project. When I say development I mean the development as well in a general sense (planning, informing, consulting, training, etc.), as in the sense of the D of R & D (Research and Development). It is not only that much work has to be done in general but also much original thinking which comes under the scope of R & D. Why co-operation in R & D?

Everyone of us knows that the bigger scientific or academic libraries of the world up till now are not at all familiar with the idea of research as it is handled now for about fifty years in industry. In industry research is done in order to keep the enterprise ahead of all other enterprises. They spend $100 million a year on research in the industrial world. An industrial enterprise has to look into the future, has to develop new methods, has to create new products and so on in order to be able to keep alive in the competition.

Such a circumstance does not exist in a scientific library. May-be this is one of the reasons why research has not yet received sufficient attention in library circles. The total expenses on library research may perhaps amount to $10 million a year. We are just now awakening to the importance of research and in several libraries or at least in several research groups some form of library research is done. But the fact remains that a library normally does not have amongst its staff people who have been appointed especially to do research work. And as research work is quite a special way of thinking, a research worker quite a special breed of scientist, it is not very likely that the people we now have in our libraries are capable of doing research work. So we have to look for new people in our libraries. These people are very scarce. And they should be paid very well in order to get brilliant ideas. So this leads us to the idea that this might very well be a reason for co-operation between libraries. It leads us into the direction of a group of research workers who work for a group of libraries and who report to that group.

Another argument for forming such a group is that it is necessary to bring together people of a great variety of basic education in a multi-disciplinary team. Mathematicians, electrical and mechanical engineers, sociologists, organizers and so on are all necessary in order to solve the problems that automation brings to libraries. Moreover there are several completely new professions created since the introduction of computers, professions that of course are not available in libraries. I refer to system analysts, system designers, programmers, coders and so on. It is far too much to ask from a library or from the board of governors of a university to appoint for that library people of all these specialities. So co-operation also here may offer a possibility. An example of group research will be described at this symposium by Mr. P. Brown, when discussing the Library of Congress Project MARC, whereby a number of libraries in the U.S.A., in Canada and in the U.K. are experimenting with a centrally provided tape. The experiments in the U.K. (Prof. E. S. Page) and in Sweden with the Medlars tape, and the experiments in the U.K. (Dr. A. K. Kent) with the C.T. and the CBAC tape, also brought before this symposium are other examples. May-be co-operation of this kind in the future can be planned at the beginning of the research project.

What is necessary, is not so much the adaption of one library to automation in the sense of transforming the daily procedures of that special library into an automated system, but to consider the library system of a country or even of the world as one whole. Our approach should be the integration of library automation on a national and an international scale. We know how librarians in charge of the bookstacks, of circulation, of descriptive cataloguing, of systematic classification and so on always have applied themselves to perfect their local systems. An enormous amount of knowledge and intellectual activity has gone into that work. It is, however, questionable whether we can continue this way and whether we should not sacrifice this perfection. If we aim at the bigger system than that of one library as such then no doubt we have to leave out personal or local perfectionism.

Automation of libraries should be treated as a part of a bigger whole, viz. the automation of information transfer in which governments, universities, research institutes and many industrial and commercial enterprises are interested. I have just to say Weinberg Report to convey what I mean. In that whole, libraries have their place.

But when we are looking in a more narrow circle, we find that it is important that libraries of universities should endeavour to develop their efforts in automation as a part of the university efforts. Libraries too long have been leading a life more or less isolated from that in their own university. They were not really incorporated in the academic life, an indispensable part of the daily research and daily teaching in the universities. All librarians fighting for the place of their library know that. But automation offers an opportunity. The research world itself is reviewing its position, its use of the mass of information produced and available. When they come to a decision, to a plan, we should be in that plan. We should seek the co-operation of our university authorities and of the teaching staff. The costs of the development of automation are so very high that it is much better to look for co-operation with other libraries. It is not only the cost of staff and of apparatus, but is is also the fact that this development and this research should be carried on through several, perhaps through many years. It is what is called in research circles "patient money." Those who invest the money, the government for instance, should know that research always needs a great deal of money during several years. We can get this money much more easily when we can show that unnecessary duplication of effort is avoided. And the available money should be spent on well-chosen projects. In this connection I should like to draw your attention to German co-operation in their institute called Zentralstelle für mechanische Dokumentation. In a certain sense the concentration of the money for library research in one place is also taking place in the United States of America where the Council on Library Resources distributes annually an amount of about $1 million among libraries and research institutes. A similar thing in a sense happens in England where through the Office for Scientific and Technical Information (OSTI) of the Department of Education and Science research of library automation is also financed.

II. STANDARDIZATION OF METHODS AND MATERIALS

All these are good arguments to organize co-operation between libraries when we are heading for automation. There is, however, another argument which comes from the nature of the machinery involved in the automation. When automation becomes a fact for libraries we have to work with apparatus that has much in common as to construction and operating methods. Of course the work with one computer varies from that with another computer, but to a large extent standardization of methods is possible and necessary and in several cases an absolute must if, for instance, national and international co-operation of libraries as to information transfer should be organized. As Mr. Merta put it in his paper: the time has come that we must consider with full seriousness the international standardization of all basic programs and arrange for compatibility.

III. CO-OPERATION IN ORDER TO ACHIEVE OUTPUT – INPUT CONNECTION

There are two points where co-operation between libraries leads to new developments.

The first one is the possibility of using computers at a distance. I feel that for us librarians this is one of the most important features of the computer of the future. It is true, as Mr. A. G. Mackenzie points out in his paper to this symposium, that a study of the actual needs of the user should have priority, and it is equally true that using computers at a distance cannot be realized to-morrow, but this should not prevent us of preparing the way for this important and desirable step. What then are for us the possibilities of using a computer at a distance?

First of all there is the possibility of getting information from other libraries. It may be information in the communication from one library to another library. But it may be also in the communication from libraries with their central library, the central library for a region or the central library for a nation. It may be that a country has a national or a regional information centre to which all other libraries and not only libraries can put their questions. It may also be that there is a central catalogue of all books, periodicals and other documents of the libraries of a country. Of course first of all we should standardize the way questions to the central institute are put. But moreover as you never can allow everyone to put questions, to use your own computer, there should be a group forming, there should be a certain level of people that are allowed to use that computer. There are of course many other things still to organize between the central institute and its users. But the fact that a great deal of work still has to be done if such co-operation is created does not mean that it should not be attempted; on the contrary it only means that we should co-operate to the fullest.

It is not only possible to ask questions to a central computer but it is also possible to introduce information into a central computer. This again may be the introducing of general information to a central information system and it may mean the contribution of titles to a central catalogue. The important point that should be kept in mind is that the output-side of one machine should be connected to the input-side of the other machine. In devising our methods in the library we should therefore always be aware of the requirements of other machines at a distance, which can determine our own systems. The second possibility for co-operating on a national and international scale that did not exist before is the sharing of information through the common use of information put on magnetic tape. Bibliographical work, indexes, library catalogues and so on, they all can be put on magnetic tape, they can be made available to any library anywhere in the world that has a computer and that asks for more information. This co-operation is as we know just in the experimental or in the organizational stage. But it is already clear now that it is not sufficient to produce magnetic tape with a wealth of information; this material has to be prepared in such a way that it can be received by other computers. We have learned through the paper of Professor Page of the amount of work done in the University of Newcastle upon Tyne, with the support of OSTI and the help of NLL. Honeywell tapes have to be converted into IBM tapes and then again to English Electric tapes. Through co-operation from the start we must for the future avoid all that converting. Of course I understand that under the circumstances we should be happy at least that a system like Medlars exists and that the testing of it in other libraries comes afterwards. May-be without the initiative of the National Library of Medicine nothing would have happened up till now. But we should aim at creating systems that are meant for many libraries in the world through a co-operative group of system designers.

IV.   NATIONAL AND INTERNATIONAL PLANNING NECESSARY TO INSURE CO-OPERATION

If automation in libraries is the important thing we think it is for the single library, for the national and for the international library system then for our own sake and for that of our users we should insist on co-operation in development, in research and in the organization of our activities for the future.

There should be developed a planning activity both on the national and on the international level, so that good guidance is given to the many and varied activities which otherwise would just grow wildly, and certainly not efficiently. Several of the papers of this symposium bear upon a national policy. Mr. Buncl deals with the building up of a Czechoslovakian information network, Mr. Dorský outlines the main trends of the Czechoslovakian research on mechanization and automation of his country's information system, Mr. Wiesenberger deals with the organization of scientific, technical and economical data, and Mr. Stefánik is concerned with the financing of the Czechoslovakian network. It is clear that Czechoslovakia tries to avoid a wild growth and that it tries to direct a co-operation effort towards a national goal. This is an example to be followed by many other countries.

THE INFLUENCE OF INFORMATION RETRIEVAL ON THE STRUCTURE OF INDEXING AND CLASSIFICATION SYSTEMS

J. TOMAN

Centre for Inventions and Scientific Information, Czechoslovak Academy of Sciences, Prague

Mr. Foskett said last May in a lecture in the Czechoslovak Academy of Sciences in Prague: "Thesaurus is a device of the Stone Age". Three weeks later during the Berlin symposium on descriptor systems several of the participants declared "The classification systems are no good, we need to construct thesauruses". The old dispute between the supporters of the classification systems and the supporters of the alphabetic, indexing systems obviously goes on as it has been going on for decades.

On the one hand there is the great work of Dr. Ranganathan and of the Classification Research Group and their contribution to the modern theory of classification, and on the other hand the sober reality — the majority of mechanized retrieval systems adopts alphabetical systems-descriptors, uniterms. If we do not want to be blind to the actual situation, we must admit that the classifications are losing ground even in the areas where they reigned for decades in the form of UDC. The situation in socialist countries such as Czechoslovakia, Poland, Hungary, German Democratic Republic and Roumania is typical. Documentation centres of these countries have been bastions of UDC for years. Hundreds of information centres in all these countries, especially in the field of technology, have been using UDC. The situation is changing at present. The introduction of punch card machines and computers brings the wave of uniterms and descriptors (thesauruses).

Years ago when I became acquainted with the works of Ranganathan, Vickery, Foskett, Cleverdon, Mills and others I started a series of popular articles and publications about the development of modern classification and indexing systems. Our lectures in the courses for the training of documentalists informed the participants about uniterms, descriptors, thesauruses, semantic factors, faceted classification, categories, integrated levels, about the polemics around UDC (Vickery, Kyle and Fill) etc.

Being persuaded that modern classification systems are better than the thesauruses I must admit that I am horrified hearing now — fortunately very rare views — that the system of UDC should be abolished and for each

57

field of science and technology a thesaurus should be constructed. The whole framework of UDC connecting hundreds of information centres would collapse and an atomization of the present coordinated net of information centres would be brought about.

We remember the criticism of the UDC which has been going on for some years. The critics were persuaded that a modern classification system should be substituted for the UDC, in their opinion obsolete. But this criticism together with the propagation of information retrieval has resulted in thesauruses being substituted for the UDC. This certainly was not the intention of the critics, who are advocates of systems of classification and not of alphabetic indexing.

What is the explanation of the fact that the majority of new systems are alphabetic and not classification systems? I think that the chief reason is that *the rules for the construction of a classification are far more complicated than for the construction of a thesaurus.* An ordinary information man has great difficulties in constructing a thesaurus for his field, not to speak of the construction of a faceted classification system.

During the discussions of the international conference on classification at Elsinore I pointed to the fact that it had limited its papers and discussions to the systems of classification and ignored the development and extension of alphabetic systems such as uniterms, descriptors (thesauruses). Why not analyse the advantages and disadvantages of both lines (directions) of organising information, of systems of indexing and classification?

What is the difference between the alphabetic (subject) and classification systems and what is common to both? Since the report on the results of the Cranfield project I tried to find an answer to this question. The authors writing about Cranfield, especially Cleverdon and Mills, offered their inspiration to this study when they spoke about different instruments which characterized the four systems examined during the Cranfield project. These allusions were not worked out further in the literature, although they represented a very interesting approach to the problems of organising information. I followed this line and tried *to analyse the elements of different systems of organising information without prejudice in favour of either classification or indexing systems.*

These studies led to an interesting result, that *each system is but another combination of organising principles and that many principles occur both in systems of classification and in systems of indexing.*

Some classification specialists prefer to distinguish other two main directions — hierarchical and nonhierarchical systems, or precoordinated and postcoordinated systems. Because most systems are characterized by some degree of hierarchy, precoordination or postcoordination, it is not easy to use these characteristics for the distinction or different systems of organizing knowledge. On the other hand when distinguishing systems of indexing and systems of classification one comes to clearer results. The distinction reflects not only the historical development (the old antagonism between these two trends), which express the contents of document. Terms can be arranged only either:

1 by the outer form of the written word (alphabet)

or 2 by the inner contents of the term

Let us call the different instruments which the indexing and the classification systems use for organising human knowledge "principles."

Which are the main principles governing the two trends of organising knowledge?

Systems of indexing are characterized by the *alphabetical principle* – the terms in the systems are arranged according to the alphabet.

Classifications are characterized by two main principles, *the principle of subject (systematic) grouping of terms* and *the principle of hierarchy*.

But even the use of these main principles is not limited to one of these trends. Alphabetic systems use a certain degree of hierarchy, and classifications use the alphabetic principle in the alphabetic index of terms.

Two other contrary principles are *the controlled and uncontrolled vocabulary*. Classification systems are governed by the principle of controlled dictionary, whereas some systems of subject headings and uniterms are using uncontrolled dictionaries. But other systems of subject headings and all thesauruses use the principle of a controlled dictionary.

Another pair of contrary principles are *the principles of an openended system and of a closed system*. These principles are connected with the preceding ones. Traditional classifications are characterized by the disadvantage of a closed system, whereas uniterms, subject headings and thesauruses are open-ended to different degrees.

Two other contrary principles are *precoordination and postcoordination*. Older systems, both alphabetic and classification systems, are characterized by precoordination, but modern ones (thesaurus, uniterms, faceted classifications) by postcoordination.

Then there are some principles which are characteristic for either alphabetic systems or classifications. The systems of classifications use *the principle of expressing terms by symbols (notation)*.

The modern systems of faceted classification use the *principle of categories*.

Last but not least let us mention *the principle of the survey of used terms*. The Cranfield project showed a simple truth, which can be expressed in a simplified manner: No system of indexing and classification can be better than its index. Some of the new systems of thesauruses use another new instrument – a displaying of associations (in the form of graphs, Euratom).

All the previous principles were concerned with the problem of organising the system itself. This last principle is concerned with the survey about the system and its contents.

It is quite natural that a system of classification possesses, beside the survey of terms in systematic order (tables), a survey of terms in an alphabet order (index). It would be quite logical that a system organised according to the alphabet should possess a survey of terms arranged systematically.

But which system of uniterms, subject headings or thesauruses possesses a systematic survey of all the terms used in the system? This is one of the greatest drawbacks of alphabetic systems. Just imagine that one comes into a universal library and would like to know which topics are represented in the file from the field of chemistry. One can only look up one term after the other in the files, but one does not find a display of terms of chemistry, physics, etc.

The study of different systems of subject organisation of human knowledge brings us to the conclusion that these use the following principles in different combinations:

alphabetic grouping	systematic grouping of terms
no hierarchy	hierarchy
uncontrolled dictionary	controlled dictionary
precoordination	postcoordination
open-ended system	closed system
notation	
categories	

display of terms used in the system (alphabetic or systematic or both) leading to a display of associations.

Are there any other principles important for the characterization of the system? I think that the above-mentioned are the principle ones. *Every system of classification and indexing is governed by a different combination of these 13 principles.* If a new system claims that it is completely different from the existing ones, it should be proved that it represents a new combination of these principles or quite a new principle not known till that time (is it possible that a completely new principle will appear in the future?).

Let us arrange the most important systems of indexing and classification in a table indicating the principles which they use.

	subject headings	uniterms	thesaurus	classification trad.	faceted
alphabetic grouping of terms	3	3	3	only in the alphabetic index	
systematic grouping of terms	1	–	1	3	3
hierarchy	1	–	2	3	2–3
no hierarchy	2	3	–		
controlled vocabulary	2	–	3	3	3
uncontrolled vocabulary	1	3	–	–	–
precoordination	3	–	–	2	–

postcoordination	–	3	3	1	3
open-ended	3	3	2	1	2
closed	–	–	1	2	1
notation				3	3
categories					3
alphabetic display of terms	–	1	3	3	3
systematic display of terms	–	–	–	3	3
display of associations			1 some		

Because the application of the different principles varies in degree, we used 1 for weak, 2 for medium and 3 for a strong application of the respective principle. It is quite clear that readers will differ in assigning the numbers, but certainly only within small limits.

To explain two examples, subject headings use some degree of hierarchy (and in consequence a certain degree of thematic grouping) for example – "libraries: special, technical, university". Traditional classifications (UDC) use to some degree postcoordination expressed by the colon. If we examine the table in detail, we see that faceted classification employs the greatest number of principles. Is this one of the proofs that it is the best system? In any case it uses principles which are necessary for a mechanized information retrieval system.

Having analysed the most important systems of indexing and classification into their principles we can proceed to judgment of the value and usefulness of the individual principles. This would allow us to build a type of system which represents the combination of all principles which we judge as necessary. Although we leave further consideration to the reader, we must stress one point – *the usefulness of different principles differs according to the purpose it serves.*

So far as I know there has been no clear and categorical statement made in literature about the different demands which the different types of records

1 bound indexes
2 files
3 punch cards and memory of the computer

make on the system of indexing and classification. I remember the time when this was not clear to me. I then accepted the general opinion that postcoordination is a far better principle than precoordination. Within one week I read two papers which struck me by their difference of opinion.

Anzalone, Brokers and Cohn in their article "A Novel Index Tailored to Plastic Specialists" (American Documentation No. 3, 1964) wrote about

the advantages of precoordination and Jeffery during the conference of
Patent offices (ICIREPAT) in 1961 praised the advantages of
postcoordination.

I pondered over the antagonism between the two quite different
statements of Anzalone and Jeffery. Both were apparently right in their
assertions: in one case precoordination presented a good account, in the
second postcoordination. But why? What was the difference between the
two cases? The answer was simple — Anzalone used a bound index and
Jeffery used machine punch cards. The first type of record demands
precoordination and the second postcoordination.

Although some authors disapprove of the use of the term "multidimensional" when speaking about the systems of indexing and classification, I
think that this term expresses well the difference between the precoordinated and postcoordinated systems. The first allows the approach to the
file only from one viewpoint, the second from several viewpoints. Let us
imagine that we have to look for a document characterized by several
terms, in a traditional file containing several hundred thousand cards. This
would be quite impossible, because the traditional file allows the approach
always only from one angle and under each viewpoint of the search
question are many records. If a record in a traditional file deals with four
terms A, B, C and D, we prepare four copies and file them under all four
terms. When we search the file we can look either under

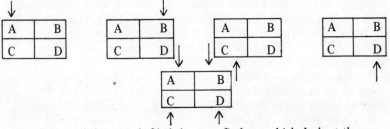

and examine all the records filed there, to find out which deals at the same
time with the other 3 terms. But when we use any type of punch cards
(peek-a-boo or edge-notched cards) we can approach the information
system from all four viewpoints simultaneously. This testifies that the
traditional file is onedimensional and the punch cards (and the memory of
the computer) multidimensional. The progress from the file to the punch
cards is so great that it can be compared only with the progress made half
a century ago, when the bound catalogue, which did not allow the filing of
new records in their alphabetical order, was replaced by the then modern
file cards.

We come to a very important conclusion: *the new medium of record
(punch cards) is multidimensional and it demands the use of a multidimensional (postcoordinated) system of indexing or classification, whereas the
traditional types of records (bound catalogue and card files) allow or prefer
the use of precoordinated systems.* The application of multidimensional

records immensely influences the theory of classification in such a manner as to do away with the difference between indexing and classification systems.

Differences between indexing and classification systems disappear when the organising system is used with a multidimensional type of record. In the previous paragraphs we came to the conclusion that just as each system of classification should offer a systematic display of terms (tables) and an alphabetic display of terms (index), each system of indexing (subject headings, uniterms, thesaurus) should use both these displays. But if we introduce both these displays, how shall we recognize whether the system used in a special case is alphabetical or a classification system? But what about the file of edge-notched cards or machine punch-cards, which are random?

We come to a second important conclusion: *The difference between indexing (alphabetic) and classification systems disappears in an information system, where multidimensional records are used.* (This is clearer in a special system of indexing or classification than in a universal one.)

Once this conclusion is accepted among the critics, another third important conclusion offers itself. *During the theoretical studies in the field of classification much less time should be devoted to the problem of the order of terms,* because in the mechanized information retrieval systems the order of terms of indexing or classification has no longer any importance.

The systems of organizing knowledge lose their purpose of organising the information in a modern retrieval system. It is an irony no doubt that an organising system loses its purpose of organising, but it seems to be true.

The order of terms is necessary only for the display of terms used in the system of indexing or classification, but not for the arrangement of the information – which was its chief purpose till yesterday. The theoretical problem of the order of terms is far less important, when it concerns only the systematic display of terms used in the system (the tables), than the order of information in the information system.

Finally we come to the fourth conclusion: *Both trends or organising systems, systems of indexing and classifications, tend to merge.*

The supporters of the thesaurus are not aware of the fact, because they have always critized the classifications and disregarded their development. On the other hand the advocates of classification systems have criticized too long the disadvantages of indexing systems and are likewise prejudiced.

But if we analyse quite impartially the development of the last 15 years in indexing (uniterms, descriptors, thesaurus, semantic factors) and in classification (Ranganathan, CRG, etc.) we cannot fail to observe the convergent lines of these two trends. The decisive point for the merge was the introduction of new medium of records which need not be arranged according to an alphabetic or systematic order, but which are random.

Analysing the situation we observe two other facts: The modern systems of indexing (semantic factors, thesaurus) are taking over the principles which are characteristic of classifications (hierarchy, categories). It seems that systems of classification should take over from thesauruses their good innovation — the display of associations. Both of the trends introduced the modern principle of postcoordination (Ranganathan 1933, Taube 1952). Beside this another development takes place:

THE SYNTHESIS OF CONTRARY PRINCIPLES

Uniterms in their original form do not use any degree of hierarchy. UDC uses a strong hierarchy of long hierarchical chains. Experience shows that both excess of hierarchy and no hierarchy is not advantageous. The truth lies in the middle — a weak hierarchy (of three to four hierarchical levels when possible) seems to be the best.

An uncontrolled vocabulary has great disadvantages, but similarly a controlled vocabulary using strictly only the prescribed terms limits its effectivity (especially in modern information retrieval systems which do not allow for browsing). It seems to me that the future development will take a new turn. Controlled terms will be used with each document for characterizing its content for the future retrieval and uncontrolled terms in detail. But these uncontrolled terms will not serve for searching. In my opinion this will be another synthesis of two contrary principles.

Although it seems that precoordination will serve better the traditional mediums of records (bound catalogues and files) and postcoordination the modern medium of records (punch cards and computer), there still remains the possibility of a synthesis. Some applications of machine punch cards in Czechoslovakia show the advantage of a combination of precoordination and postcoordination even in mechanised retrieval systems. If a combination of two (or three) terms occurs very often, why not simplify the search by using the precoordinated combination of terms on the one hand and in the same time post the number of the document also under the individual terms of this complex term? For instance why not use precoordination by employing the descriptor "circulation of journals" and postcoordination by employing also the terms "circulation" and "journals"?

Finally we come to the last two main principles characterizing the two trends of indexing and classification — the principles of alphabetic and systematic grouping of terms. A synthesis of these two contrary principles will certainly seem quite unthinkable both to adherents of indexing and to adherents of classification. Returning to the conclusions of the previous paragraphs, we realize that the order of terms loses its importance. Why not combine alphabetic grouping with thematic?

In the faceted classification with mnemonic notation used in the project INDORES in the Czechoslovak Academy of Sciences we use a combination of both these principles. The four categories are divided into facets, which are arranged according to the alphabet of their (mostly) mnemonic notation. The terms in the facets are arranged according to the alphabet. Thus the principle of thematic grouping was merged with the principle of alphabetic grouping. The system retains the advantages of a classification, and removes some of its disadvantages connected with the building of the system. Introducing new terms into the system is very easy.

There is a question how to name this system. According to one's sympathies one can call it an alphabetic classification or a classified thesaurus. If we accept the notion of an indexing or a classification system as a combination of fundamental principles in various combinations, then we can experiment more easily with the principles themselves and with their combinations than we were able till now, when every organising system represented separate entity for us. We shall be able to move the qualities of two contrary principles nearer together in order to achieve the right synthesis. Similarly we shall have less inhibitions about taking over principles which worked well in another system.

We came in our consideration to two other conclusions: The fifth conclusion: *Systems of indexing and classification tend to take over the principles used up to now in the other trend of organising knowledge.* The sixth conclusion: *Contrary principles tend to merge in a synthesis which improves the qualities of these principles.*

FUTURE TASKS

The gradual propagation of mechanized retrieval systems is connected with new organising systems for different fields of science and technology. To facilitate the creation of these systems, simple rules should be established which would enable to produce faceted (or alphabetic faceted) classifications which are more advanced than the thesaurus.

The problem of a universal classification is long-term and too serious to be attacked before the problem of special classification. If the efforts were concentrated for years on the creation of a universal classification, it could happen that it would be finished only in the moment when the whole world would have adopted thesauruses.

The principles of indexing and classification should be examined in detail to find out their influence on the quality of information systems. Different combinations of various principles should be tried out in practice to determine the best systems for different purposes. The differences of the influence of onedimensional and multidimensional records on the system of indexing and classification should be analysed.

Special attention should be devoted to the problem of associations (related terms) and their role in improving the results of retrieval.

SUMMARY OF CONCLUSIONS

Every system of indexing or classification is a combination of different fundamental principles.

Most of these principles appear in the systems of both indexing and classification.

The new medium of record (punch cards) is multidimensional and demands the use of a multidimensional (postcoordinated) system of index-ing or classification, whereas the traditional types of records (bound catalogue and card files) prefer the use of precoordinated (onedimensional) systems of indexing or classification.

The difference between indexing and classification systems disappears in an information system, where multidimensional records are used.

Because the problem of the order of terms disappears in mechanized systems, it loses its importance in theoretical studies.

Both trends of organising systems, indexing and classification systems, tend to merge.

Systems of indexing and classification tend to take over principles previously used in the other trend of organising knowledge.

Contrary principles tend to merge in a synthesis which improves the qualities of these principles.

Because these conclusions are the results of an analysis and considera-tions of an individual, they should be examined critically into their correctness.

Footnote:

Because there was felt to be a lack of a term standing as a broader term above the terms "indexing systems" (alphabetical systems) and "classification systems" the author employed the term "organising systems". Likewise the term "ordering systems" could be used, but this could eventually cause a misunderstanding because of the different meanings of the term "to order". In the Czech language the exact translation of "ordering system" is being used. Similarly in German "Ordnungssystem" stands above "Schlagwortsysteme" and "Klassifikationssysteme".

STRUCTURE IN CLASSIFICATION AND INDEXING SYSTEMS

D. J. FOSKETT

University of London Institute of Education

The topic of structure in classification and indexing systems is one that illustrates quite well the spiral of history. When the first modern system of bibliographical classification was published by Dewey in 1876, it inaugurated an era of new general schemes that lasted, in its inspirational phase, until 1933, when Ranganathan published the first edition of the Colon Classification. One cannot, unfortunately, regard any edition of CC as a worthy representative of analytico-synthetic classification, and I shall take the final published version of the Bibliographic Classification, ending in 1953, as the peak of performance of the "enumerative" era. Trends antagonistic to classification, as exemplified by the great enumerative schemes, were already at work by that time; punched card systems, manual and automatic, were well-known, and in the first flush of enthusiasm for the abolition of filing catalogue cards in a pre-determined sequence, both classified and alphabetical orders were completely replaced by random sorting. The mechanism through which any entry was retrieved did not require the distasteful and laborious task of putting the index entries in one, and only one, correct sequence.

It has come to be realised, however, that a retrieval mechanism is not all there is to an information handling system. Even where the extracting device itself does not rely on order, some form of internal organisation is usually seen to be forced upon an indexing language, for other reasons. In this paper, I want to explore some of these reasons; I shall quote actual examples of structure, but my intention is to attempt an analytical rather than a descriptive approach. This is not, of course, to say that descriptions of instances are unnecessary; the whole of the classificatory sciences are founded on such descriptions. But there comes a time when any field of study, if it is to call itself systematic, or scientific, has to derive, from its instances, principles and hypotheses that can indicate future developments. We do not have to stand and wait for additional instances to turn up before we can advance knowledge.

I believe that this approach is of particular importance in the field of information retrieval at this moment. Indeed, I believe that the term "information retrieval" itself has come to be used quite wrongly, to denote the whole of the process of acquiring new knowledge from a store. I have no alternative term to offer, but I want to emphasise that the process of "information retrieval" actually constitutes only a part of the overall activity of documentation. Information Retrieval means two things: it means (1) that "information" is meaningful, and (2) that it has previously been lodged in the store.

These two apparently simple statements actually comprehend a number of complex notions and processes. To analyse them fully would be beyond the scope of a single essay, but it will have to be done if we want to end the present proliferation of so-called systems that look wonderful on paper, and require all sorts of expensive machines, but which finally give the user an even more indifferent service than he had before. We have now, I consider, to look beyond the mere description of systems, and examine their purposes. All too often these purposes have been forgotten; systems have come to be prized, not for what they do, but for how they do it — the means have been turned into the ends, as if moving a bit of information from one place to another is all that is required.

There has been some confusion with what is called "Information Theory", the subject that has grown out of telephone engineering and is involved with the transmission of messages. The confusion arises out of two major factors: (1) the messages to be transmitted are complete, and therefore precisely circumscribed and known, and (2) the transmitting process has nothing to do with the meaning of the message; the consequence of this is that an important aspect of information theory is the elimination of redundancy, or "noise". Neither of these factors applies in our field of information handling, but the unplanned production of systems for dealing with information in documents has resulted in the creation of models as if they were factories for the transmission of messages, in which the raw material, after being processed, remains the same raw material because all that has happened is that it has been moved from one place, the store, to another, the user. Marks made on one piece of paper have been processed by writing, punching holes in cards or tape, or magnetising spots on a metal strip, in order to make the same marks on another piece of paper.

It is my contention that documentation is concerned with more than moving marks on paper from here to there. There is a difference, surely, between a clerk in a telegraph office and a librarian or documentalist. It is not for nothing that such words as "relevance" and "pertinence" have come into our literature, and the distinction between these two is of great significance. Anyone who has actually worked in a library knows that the bibliographical data are only a part of the story. We have to understand the needs of the enquirer, we have to bring his statement of these needs into relation with the subject field, and to organise the search of our store so that the documents we provide will be as helpful as possible. The notions of "relevance" to a subject (that which has public recognition as a part of that subject), and "pertinence" to an enquiry (that which will resolve the enquirer's difficulty) both depend on the recognition of information by the human mind. The distinction between then lies in the fact that, in the one case, the information relates to the subject in a fully public way that would be generally acknowledged by experts in the field; while in the other case, the information relates to the subject in a way that has a bearing on one particular situation. Obviously the two notions need not be mutually exclusive, but in the particular situation the marks on paper that represent pertinent information could not be replaced by another set of marks conveying different information, even though that information also has public recognition in the general sense. Pertinent information has been transformed from simple information by an act of judgement, and it has thus been accorded a totally new status; it has become knowledge, the intellectual possession of a human being. Information, as Professor Michael Oakeshott has pointed out, is "the explicit ingredient of knowledge, where what we know may be itemised". When we speak of "information" as such, we are not discussing its status in respect of any particular situation, we are merely enumerating the statements that it consists of — the facts that are the publicly-recognised answers to specific questions: "What time is the next train to Manchester?", "Who won the World Cup?", "What was the date of the Battle of Waterloo?", "What is the molecular structure of polythene?", and so on.

Information is the explicit ingredient of knowledge, but only when a human mind gets to work on it does it become knowledge. Of itself, information is neither useful nor useless, but no knowledge is useless or existing for its own sake; the very fact that it is *knowledge* — a piece of knowing — means that a human mind has recognised it and understood it as having significance for a particular purpose.

Now there are three important ways in which knowledge can be discussed: as to its nature, the philosophical aspect; as to how it may be acquired, the psychological aspect; as to the naming of it, the linguistic aspect. In recent years notable contributions have been made in all these areas, particularly in respect of teaching and learning, and even though we may not claim to be teachers, as documentalists we are surely concerned to see that our systems help people to learn. We should not answer "1815" to the question "Who won the World Cup?", not because the status of the statement that Waterloo was fought in 1815 is in any way changed, but because it is simply irrelevant as an answer to this question. I suppose you might also say that it is impertinent, because it certainly does not help our enquirer to learn anything, and the reason is that its information has no place in the scheme of knowledge that he has under consideration at this time.

The very fact that we can thus accord to an item of information a status of "relevant" or "irrelevant" signifies that we are not considering it by itself, but in relation to other items that we already have in our possession. We are, moreover, able to set up criteria of judgement; on being given an item, we can say whether or not we should take it up and apply it to the matter in hand. How are we able to do this?

Whatever theory of knowledge we may subscribe to, science itself demands that we accept the preliminary proposition that there is a universe of real phenomena, existing apart from ourselves — "out there", so to speak — and that we can investigate these phenomena and manipulate them in such a way as to bring about results that we have determined in advance. We are able to acquire and exercise some control over our environment — to such an extent, indeed, that we are now capable of destroying it utterly and ourselves along with it. Even those who claim that all we can know are our own sensations act in accordance with the belief that there can be agreement with others on the nature of these sensations, and they accept that a public consensus can exist; they are usually ready to accept such a consensus even on matters of which they have no direct experience, such as the dates of historical events or the predictive accuracy of railway time-tables. In being able to accept a public consensus, and to engage in purposeful action here and now, what we are doing is to accept that the items of information we constantly receive can be built up into a scheme which has intrinsic consistency; if it did not, our expectations would never be fulfilled, and we should never know what was going to happen next. We depend, in other words, on the belief that reality has structure and that we can grasp it with our minds. As Professor Paul Hirst has put it, "to have a 'rational mind' certainly implies experience structured under some form of conceptual schema".

The concern of the documentalist, however, is not so much with reality as with documents. We have therefore to recognise, as Fairthorne has often reminded us, the distinction between an entity and a description of it. There is a big difference between playing tennis and reading how to play tennis. But to play tennis is to have acquired the skill to put the rules of tennis into practical effect, and if we did not know the rules we could not hope to play the game properly. Reading the rules may not make us good players, but it enables us to understand the game — that is, to form a conceptual scheme by means of which we know what it is when we see a tennis court and tennis being played. It will also help us to avoid playing the game wrongly. The purpose of a document, whether descriptive or prescriptive, is to enhance the understanding of its reader, and it does this by indicating the structure of what it describes, the constituent entities and the relations between them.

This is one side of the question. Understanding has to be conveyed. It also has to be grasped. We have come a long way since the days when philosophers like John Locke wrote of the child's mind as a blank slate, *tabula rasa,* on which a teacher inscribed what he considered to be knowledge. Even in Locke's own time, of course, Comenius was laying the foundations of modern ideas of education with his Pansophic School in which the ability to perform was as important as the knowledge of things. "What they are to know must then be supplemented by what they are to do; and we desire our pupils to be trained in this respect, so that the ability to perform is added to knowledge of the matter". Modern work on concept formation shows that the young child learns mainly from direct experience, from sensori-motor activities which enable him to build up logical and classificatory systems. In these systems, information derived from observing and noting certain features such as redness, and roundness comes to be associated with information from activities such as peeling and chewing, and the result is the formation of a concept in the mind, which is fixed by giving it a name: this is an orange. To have a concept of X means more than simply to have been informed that "X is X"; it means that we have made to ourselves an explication of X in terms which we already possess. The ability to do this depends on having a structure, a conceptual scheme, already in our minds.

The communication of knowledge, therefore, constitutes an act through which a structured scheme of data becomes assimilated, to use Piaget's term, into the mind of a learner, who adjusts his existing scheme so as to accommodate what is new in the data communicated. The medium by which this transference takes place is language, and it is no accident that the study of linguistics has been completely transformed by such scholars as de Saussure, Vygotsky and Luria, Hjelmslev and Halliday, whose approaches are based on social and psychological rather than on purely historical grounds. They point out that even when the significance of a concept has been grasped – as when the child knows how to peel and eat an orange – verbalisation constitutes a further step because language itself has an intrinsic structure that has to be grasped. In this it is different from all other fields of study (except perhaps classification) in that while it is a phenomenon *sui generis* with its own rules and consistency, it is also the medium by which we come to know of the rule and structures of other phenomena.

Language is involved in communication in two ways. First, it is used by a writer to describe what he takes to be the reality he is concerned with; and second, it is used by the reader to apprehend and fix the new concepts he is reading about. One way of telling whether or not we have understood a new idea is to try to explain it in our own words. Experimental studies on normal and handicapped children, by Furth and Milgram, have attempted to clarify the role of verbal factors in both description and classification, and have shown that while a child may be observed to have classified a concept correctly, he may still find difficulty in expressing his classification in words.

This type of difficulty is very familiar to librarians. All of us know how hard it is for a reader to state his needs accurately, unless he is asking a specific question that has a specific answer – unless, that is, he is requiring a simple transfer of information. That this should be so goes to confirm that there is more to documentation than simple transfers of information. My thesis is that information systems should not be limited to factual statements, but should be considered, as Ranganathan claimed, as artificial "languages", into which statements made in natural language about reality may be transformed for incorporation into accessible stores. Such a language would need to have internal structure and rules for operation; and the closer such structure approximated to the structure of real phenomena, the longer it would last and the more successful it would be in facilitating the communication of knowledge.

Translated into the terms of documentation, this means that a structure should be built into an indexing language; that this implies some pre-coordination of terms, plus rules for post-coordination; and that there is a pattern of reality itself which the structure of the indexing language should imitate. I maintain that these factors are more important than ever in the era of mechanised information handling, and that this is recognised by information engineers, however dimly, in their resuscitation of the idea of a "thesaurus". Some even talk of a "structured thesaurus", as if the usual thesaurus had no structure; this is necessary because some of those produced actually have little, certainly nothing like the original elaborate classification of Roget.

To illustrate how structure has been built into a modern thesaurus, let us compare certain terms from MESH — the Medical Subject Headings used by the highly advertised and successful MEDLARS — with a similar group taken from the Library of Congress List of Subject Headings, compiled some fifty years ago (Figure 1).

Library of Congress	MESH
	Category A Anatomical Terms
	A1 Parts of the Body
Face	
sa Chin	FACE
Mouth	Eye (A9)
xx Head	Mouth (A3)
Diseases	
	LIPS (A3)
Lips	
	MOUTH (A3)
Mouth	Lips (A3)
sa Jaw	Tongue (A3)
Lips	
Tongue	TONGUE (A3)
xx Face	
Head	
— Diseases	A3 Digestive System
Taste	MOUTH (A1)
xx Senses and Sensation	Lips (A1)
Tongue	Tongue (A1)
	TASTE BUDS (A9)
Tongue	
sa Taste	TONGUE (A1)
xx Mouth	Taste Buds (A9)
— Cancer	

Fig. 1

It can easily be seen that we have some development from the LC List, which includes Whole-Part and Whole-Process terms in the same array; in MESH the Process terms have been left out. This is because a new structural element has been added: the arrangement of the terms in a series of categories. Anatomical terms are to be found in Category A, Diseases in Category C. This arrangement in categories opens up a whole new series of relationships, because at each term we find not only a group derived from one characteristic, such as Whole-Part, but a reference in brackets to the other groups in which the term may figure. This is a tacit recognition, absent from the LC List, that the structure of reality is a series of classifications — a lattice system — and not a single hierarchy. On the other hand, as Figure 2 shows, the itemising of terms in the categories is sometimes remarkably haphazard. Thus in Category C 5, PNEUMOCONIOSIS includes Silicosis and also Anthracosilicosis and Silicotuberculosis, both of which appear again under SILICOSIS and are "species" of it. In Category C 14, the lists under OCCUPATIONAL DISEASES and POISONING show no clarity of thought whatever.

C DISEASES
C5 — Respiratory Diseases

PNEUMOCONIOSIS (C14)	SILICOSIS
Anthracosilicosis	Anthracosilicosis
Silicosis	Silicotuberculosis
Silicotuberculosis (C1)	

C14 Injury, Poisoning (etc)

OCCUPATIONAL DISEASES (C16)	POISONING
Agricultural Workers' Diseases	CO Poisoning
Decompression Sickness	CCl_4 Poisoning
Lead Poisoning	Food Poisoning
Occupational Dermatitis	Gas Poisoning
Pneumoconiosis (C5)	Lead Poisoning
	Mercury Poisoning
PNEUMOCONIOSIS (C5)	....

Fig. 2

But that there has been something of an attempt to find the intrinsic logic of the subject can be seen by comparing the list of categories in MESH with those of the faceted classification for Occupational Safety and Health used by the Centre International de Sécurité in the International Labour Organisation in Geneva. (Figure 3)

Allowing for the different subject coverage of the two systems, there is sufficient similarity here to show that the compilers of MESH have recognised the basis of facet analysis, which is of course a deliberate attempt to create categories on a logical foundation.

F

MEDICAL SUBJECT HEADINGS MESH Categories		CIS Facets	
A	Anatomical Terms	B	Physical agents and natural phenomena
B	Organisms	C–G	Substances
C	Diseases	C	Inorganic chemicals
D	Chemicals and Drugs	D	Organic chemicals
E	Analytical, Diagnostic and Therapeutic Technics and Equipment	F–G	Natural products and industrial substances
F	Psychiatry and Psychology	H–J	Premises, equipment, operations, processes
G	Biological Sciences		
H	Physical Sciences	K	Types of work and industrial organisation
I	Social Sciences		
J	Technology, Commerce and Industry	L	Fires and explosions
		M–N	Pathology
K	Humanities	P	Physiology and Psychology
L	Communication, Library Science and Documentation	Q	Methods of investigation
		R	Medical prevention and treatment
M	Named Groups of People	S	Safety and health engineering
		T	Personal protective equipment
		V	Safety and health organisation
		W	Groups of persons
		X	Industries
		Y, Z	General

Fig. 3

The necessity of a structured arrangement can also be shown by an examination of that very popular form of index, the Keyword-in-Context. I should like to compare a KWIC index in Comparative Education produced at the University of Michigan with the *Index Radiohygenicus;* both use a KWIC index, but in one significantly different way. The *Comparative Education Index* has the following entries:

SCHOOLS AT HOME AND	ABROAD
EDUCATIONAL TRENDS	ABROAD
NTRY SCHOOL AT HOME AND	ABROAD. THE COU
NCE OF GERMAN EDUCATION	ABROAD. VALUE AND INFLUE
EDUCATION IN EMERGING	AFRICA
EDUCATION IN LATIN	AMERICA
STUDIES IN	FOREIGN EDUCATION
ERICAN DISSERTATIONS ON	FOREIGN EDUCATION. AM
EACHERS OF ENGLISH AS A	FOREIGN LANGUAGE. ANNOTATED BIBLIOG
PARTNERSHIP IN	OVERSEA EDUCATION
EDUCATION IN	PACIFIC COUNTRIES

and many other similar entries under these and other "country" words. There are no cross references to link any of these headings, and the important book by E. J. King, *Other Schools and Ours,* which deals with several countries, appears only under SCHOOLS. In a second Michigan index on *Education in India,* the editor makes the significant remark: "It is the basic premise of all such indexes that the user will be alert to alternative ways of looking up items. Since the extremely expensive task of conventional indexing to control synonyms and provide 'see' and 'see also' references has been eliminated, the user must actively engage in such cross-checking himself". In fact, the only way in which a user can be sure that he has overlooked no heading is to read through the entire index.

If we now turn to Index Radiohygienicus, we can find the following entries:

```
                            ADOLESCENTS EXPOSED TO ATOMIC BOMB   395 1 JE
CENTS EXPOSED TO ATOMIC     BOMB./                     ADOLES   395 1 JE
OF THE MORTALITY OF A-      BOMB SURVIVORS. 3. DESCRIPTION OF THE 408 1 JE
D IONIZING RADIATION IN     JAPAN./                  LEUKEMIA AN 410 1 JE
                    APAN./  LEUKEMIA AND IONIZING RADIATION IN J 410 1 JE
ESCRIPT STUDIES OF THE      MORTALITY OF A-BOMB SURVIVORS. 3.D   408 1 JE
HE MORTALITY OF A-BOMB      SURVIVORS. 3. DESCRIPTION OF THE SAM 408 1 JE
```

These relate to three items on the same subject; the only link in the KWIC index is that two happen to appear under BOMB. There are no entries for these, though there are for other items, under IRRADIATION or RADIATION (for reasons explained in the Introduction), and there is no entry at all for a fourth article on "Irradiation in utero", number 396, which is an important editorial comment on 395. But in making a search, all these would be found fairly easily, because the bibliography itself is classified in categories, unlike the Michigan bibliographies, which are arranged in alphabetical order of authors' names, and all the above entries appear in the same opening (pp. 44–45) of the book. Used in this way, the failure of the KWIC index to act as an efficient index (pointing to useful items) is made good by the scheme of classification.

It seems to me to be completely contrary to all the principles of good indexing to throw the onus back to the user, and to provide nothing for him in the way of guides to help him in his search. The value of such guides has, I think, been proved by an interesting paper submitted to the 1964 meeting of the American Documentation Institute by Barbara A. Montague; this paper also shows clearly the confusion existing in the United States over the nature of "classification". Three systems were tested, A and B being "coordinate indexes", and C a "classification index". System A was superior to B, and both far superior to C. What made System A superior to B were 1 its system of vocabulary control, 2 its ability to provide for generic search, and 3 its superior use of rôles. As to 2, I should like to emphasise Miss Montague's own words: "the main factor responsible for irrelevance in system A occurred in one question for *which a selective generic class was not available,* and the classes which had to be searched *included concepts unrelated to the question".* Now system C is described only as "a subject index with one or two cross references on abstract cards".

Yet, in the conclusion, this apparently alphabetical list, with its meagre one or two references, has become a "classification system". Miss Montague seems to have no idea that a faceted classification is actually a controlled vocabulary, with generic structure, with precise rôles, and with selective generic classes for all of its terms. Thus her article will certainly be quoted as proof for claims which it in fact proves to be false.

As is well known, the Classification Research Group has for long agreed on the necessity for a well-integrated structure in indexing and classification systems. It has made several faceted schemes for specific subjects, some of which have been published, but lately most of our discussions have been taken up with a new general scheme. Our work progresses slowly, because while no funds can be found for this project, we are continually being asked to advise and help in the construction of more special schemes; and we believe that this kind of work would be greatly simplified if our plans for a basic general scheme could be realised.

So far as it has gone, the CRG has been studying the use of the theory of integrative levels as a base on which a scheme for the whole of knowledge might be built up. We are exploring the idea of forming a sequence of levels of entities in the first place, to see whether it is possible to assign to each entity a place in the sequence where it first emerges as a unique whole, more than the mere sum of its parts, having, in Farradane's phrase, a unique definition. This idea has been applied in detail to Geology, Mining and Sculpture, as being three subjects from different areas of knowledge (Science, Technology, Fine Art) which have nevertheless some kind of relation between them. The theory has been applied in outline to Physics, Chemistry and Politics, and works satisfactorily for Entities, which may be regarded as having a concrete existence. We are not so certain about levels of Abstractions, but have only made a preliminary survey in this area. It has been of great interest to us to see how this theory has also become very familiar in philosophy and science, though it has a very respectable ancestry, as Brian Vickery mentioned. Recent works of particular interest have been those of Oliver Reiser, Michael Polanyi, and especially James K. Feibleman; in Poland, Oskar Lange, in his *Wholes and Parts*, has discussed the relevance of the idea to the general theory of dialectical materialism, tracing the development of a chain of material systems, or "wholes", which grow by an accretion of attributes from fundamental particles up to human societies, or "to be more precise, various historical social formations". Each system comprises a group of "wholes", made up from units of the previous level but having new properties and new modes of behaviour arising from the network of relations established between members of an aggregate of units, and which transform the aggregate of entities on one level into a single unified entity on another.

The CRG has been concerned with two researches which illustrate the application of the theory to the construction of a general classification scheme, those of Mrs. Helen Tomlinson, who has studied the chain of entities, and of Mr. J. E. Farradane, who has been continuing his work on relational analysis. Our aim is not so much to produce a new scheme of the pattern of UDC or even of Colon, but a structured vocabulary of terms which could be drawn on for marginal fields in making a special scheme. We certainly believe that a new general scheme would find many applications, in general bibliographies and the catalogues of large libraries, for example; but we also hope that our method, when the research has been completed, could enable individual documentation centres to fit together parts of the scheme of terms which were relevant, and that they would be able to find in it not only all the terms they needed but also a structural analysis — a relational network — that would help them to come to a deeper understanding of their own field. If we succeed, the application of the scheme would be independent of the mechanism of retrieval, and would suit the largest national centres and the small personal index; and because, perhaps for the first time, the scheme would be based both on a scientific approach to reality and on a technique enabling that reality to be expressed in symbols, we hope that it would indeed make a universal classification in every sense of both those words.

REFERENCES

ARCHAMBAULT, R.D. *Editor — Philosophical analysis and education.* Routledge and Kegan Paul, 1965.

FEIBLEMAN, J. K. — 'Theory of integrative levels'. *British Journal for the Philosophy of Science,* Vol. 5, No. 17, 1954, pp. 59—66.

FURTH, H. G. *and* MILGRAM, N. A. — 'The influence of language on classification'. *Genetic Psychology Monographs,* vol. 72, 1965, pp. 317—351.

HIRST, P. H. — 'Liberal education and the nature of knowledge.' In: Archambault, *vide supra,* pp. 113—138.

-*idem-* 'The logical and psychological aspects of teaching.' In: Peters, *vide infra,* pp. 44—60.

LANGE, Oskar, — *Wholes and parts: a general theory of system behaviour.* Pergamon Press/PWN Warsaw, 1965.

OAKESHOTT, Michael. *Learning and teaching.* In: Peters, *vide infra,* pp 156—176.

PETERS, R. S. *Editor — The Concept of Education.* Routledge and Kegan Paul, 1967.

POLANYI, Michael. — *Science and man's place in the universe.* In: Woolf, Harry, *Editor. Science as a cultural* force. Baltimore, John Hopkins Press, 1964.

REISER, Oliver L. — *The integration of human knowledge.* Boston, Peter Sargent, 1958.

VICKERY, Brian — *Classification and indexing in science.* Butterworth, 2nd edition, 1959.

CLASSIFICATION AND THESAURI IN STRUCTURAL MECHANICS: REQUIREMENTS OF A MODERN SYSTEM OF INDEXING IN STRUCTURAL MECHANICS.

DUSAN FRANCU

Institute of Construction and Architecture
Slovak Academy of Sciences, Bratislava.

It is proposed to submit here the considerations preceding the choice of a descriptor system of indexing in the field of structural mechanics.

UNIVERSAL DECIMAL CLASSIFICATION – A CHILD OF ITS ERA

In spite of the statement of the authors of the UDC that there is no philosophical system underlying to this classification, and that its motives were merely practical, the closed system reflects admirably the atmosphere in science and philosophy prevailing at the end of the last century. It was a period of contentment, inspired by a feeling of closeness, finiteness, well known from Mr. Bernal's *Science in History,* and characterized by Stefan Zweig in the following terms: "It was a golden age of security ... The nineteenth century in its liberalistic idealism, was honestly convinced that it is under way directly and infallibly to the "best of all worlds".

Science seemed to be at the summit of success. Its magnificent building seemed to be roughly finished. It is true that people in laboratories did not fully share this optimism, but such is always the difference between men deep in books and men enjoying victory after a series of failures and disappointments. Discoveries as those of Becquerel (1896), Rutherford (1900), and Einstein (1905) did not haunt the minds of men with their far-reaching consequences in science.

THE RISE OF STRUCTURAL MECHANICS AS A SCIENCE AND A POWERFUL TOOL

Structural mechanics was no exception to the rule. This applied science was fed, like so many other technical or engineering sciences, by the vast experience accumulated by architects and builders in the course of many centuries, and by the successful attempts of scientists to elucidate the behaviour of structures, their parts and their combinations in terms of mathematical analysis of certain phenomena such as statical equilibrium, stability, elastic behaviour, and the strength of structures under the action of loads. In addition to a number of famous builders designing by making use of experience and inspiration, there is a number of names, famous in the evolution of science, such as Galilei, Hooke, Euler, Leibnitz, Coulomb, Napier, Poisson, Bernoulli, Gauchy, etc. who had prepared the great achievements of the nineteenth century builders and civil engineers whose father was Coulomb, a famous scientist and civil engineer in one person. It is natural that, without the contribution of discoveries made in other fields of science, e.g. in hydraulics, chemistry, metallurgy, etc. the arrival of the era of steel and reinforced concrete is inconceivable. Structural mechanics gave the civil engineer and builder a tool allowing a "more rational design of the structures and thus made it possible to cope with extensive and difficult structural tasks in an economic way without prejudice to safety requirements". This quotation from Straub's *History of Civil Engineering* expresses at the same time the eternal contradiction between requirements of safety and those of economy.

Thus the applied science of structural mechanics is supplying now the necessary methods for the design of structures, namely the analytical, graphic, or the numerical methods for the design of structural elements, as e.g. framed structures, especially beams, rigid frames and complicated trusses, arches and vaults, some cases of plates, and three dimensional and bulky structures stressed by tension, compression, shear, bending almost exclusively in the elastic range of behaviour of structural materials (See e.g. R. Salinger: *Praktische Statik,* 1921, after lectures given in 1909–1910).

It is true that the 18th and the 19th centuries have witnessed the birth of the theory of elasticity (Cauchy, Kirchhoff, Saint-Venant, Love, Lamé, etc.) allowing a closer approximation to the actual behaviour of structures, but the authors of the UDC seem to be aware only of pure mechanics (531), the strength of materials and the structure of matter (539), of civil engineering (624/628), and the traditional building trades (69) in addition to architecture (72) which is considered a different subject distinct from civil engineering.

CHARACTERISTIC FORMS OF SCIENCE EVOLUTION IN MODERN TIMES

The UDC was a respect-inspiring achievement especially for its universality, maintained by an elaborate system and procedure of extensions and corrections. These measures cannot, however, cope with the rigid frame of the system itself, which, I am afraid, is no longer conformable to recent trends of evolution in modern science.

The importance of scientific research increased immensely, and so did its prestige and the number of people engaged in research.

More and more detailed specialization in science and technology is accompanied by generating new interconnections between the individual branches of science and technology, allowing thus mutual fertilization, inspiration in the field of procedures and equipment, as well as in conceptions.

Numerous boundary disciplines have proved to be of immense importance for the study of complicated problems. It is hardly imaginable to maintain the traditional conceptions of individual sciences of study, methods of study, and resulting knowledge. Problems are attacked by teams of scientists combining their efforts to study the phenomenon from as many aspects as possible.

The evolution of sciences has registered a number of fundamental changes of views casting a new light on problems that had resisted the attempts of scientists using hitherto existing methods. The birth of cybernetics (Wiener) or of quantum mechanics (Planck) may be cited as examples.

NEW GOALS AND METHODS OF STRUCTURAL MECHANICS

Improved methods of production allowing a more economic and a more homogeneous production, justify the endeavour to increase both the theoretical and the experimental accuracy of structural analysis. The inventory of experimental methods used for stress analysis has increased many times since the beginning of this century, and so did the techniques of materials testing. The previously accepted approximations are no longer considered satisfactory, and the aim of new non-linear mechanics is to describe the true behaviour of structures. Neither are other simplifying assumptions tolerated. Structures are regarded as anisotropic, non-homogeneious, anelastic, varying in time, cooperating with other structural elements, and conceived with them as a whole. Static loads, acting on the structures, must often be regarded as dynamic and as such as cause dynamic affects. The problem of safety itself is regarded from a new viewpoint using the theory of probability. Slender structural elements resulting from this refined procedure of structural analysis cause new problems of stability and vibration.

The immensely advanced method of mathematical analysis supported by powerful computing machines, allow the application of exact approach methods to new problems, that had earlier been solved by trial-and-error, by empirical formulae, or had been left to experimental treatment. New symbolic methods of mathematical expressions, as e.g. the vector and tensor analyses, allow a simplification of expressions.

Structural mechanics is confronted with certain problems, resulting mostly from the slenderness of the designed elements, which are common with the problems of machine-designing, ship-building, air-craft, and instrument-designing etc.

Newly developed exact methods of economic calculations inspire direct methods of approach to the problem of optimum design.

A great concern for the results of the investigations of the structure of materials, which should allow us to foretell the behaviour of structures in terms of intermolecular forces, represents another facet of development of modern structural mechanics.

THE DRAWBACKS AND VIRTUES OF UDC WITH SPECIAL REGARD TO STRUCTURAL MECHANICS

Civil engineering, considered today as an application of structural mechanics, is dispersed in the tables of UDC in a number of classes (634, 625, 626, 627, 69). The solution of mechanical problems is necessarily separated from their physical premises and from the mathematical methods of their treatment (not to speak of the mechanized methods of solution). Similar methods of solution, and similar problems involved in mechanical engineering, air-craft design, or ship-design, are to be found in separate classes. It is difficult, or even impossible, to adjust the present UDC structure to these requirements. The refinement of classification by the use of auxiliaries creates a fringe of items dispersed in increasingly numerous groups and subgroups. This system of indexing is hardly suitable for mechanized storage or retrieval. Its universality is, of course, an important factor in international cooperation of information and library centres. The vast amount of intelectual work spent in the course of the past 50 years on extensions and the adjustment of UDC, is an asset not be wasted. Information centres adopting thesauri as a basis for mechanized retrieval will be obliged to find some tool permitting similar interconnection of their files.

ADVANTAGES EXPECTED FROM THE USE OF DESCRIPTOR SYSTEMS IN STRUCTURAL MECHANICS. ANTICIPATED DRAWBACKS.

A combination of descriptors used for the same concepts in various branches of science and technology is expected to enable a unified approach to similar problems and their solution. In particular the mathematical approach and the endeavour to use computing machines, will be correlated to the problems of structural mechanics in this multi-dimensional system of indexing. This system is hoped to improve the chances of relating the problems of structural mechanics to their physical premises (connection with the fields of other sciences and the various branches of technology).

The thesaurus will have to be set up. This requires a lot of work, which is spared to the users of UDC. In addition, it will have to be continuously revised and adjusted without the benefit of pooled experience on the part of the UDC users, organized by the FID. There are certain unsolved problems connected with the treatment of super-ordinated and subordinated concepts, with the elimination of a number of undesirable combination of descriptors. Anyway, it is believed that its use, when proper study has been given to it, and the necessary experience has been acquired, will be able to present a better means of information storage and retrieval for modern science and technology than it has been in the case of the UDC.

CENTRALLY PREPARED CATALOGUING DATA

PETER BROWN

Bodleian Library, Oxford.

Centrally prepared cataloguing records have been available for a very long time, particularly in the form of printed catalogue cards, and they have done something to reduce the amount of independent cataloguing of more or less the same books in every library. But the restrictions imposed by the distribution of catalogue records in the form of cards are well known to us all: the physical matching of the books in a library and the catalogue cards obtained from a central card distributing institution is not only a tedious manual task, but also leads to problems in the storage of books awaiting cards and of cards that may one day in the future be matched by books. Moreover, even when the cards have been matched with the corresponding books, there is a considerable amount of processing still to be done: some cards require modifications to the basic description to give correct information about the copies of books in a particular library; added headings have to be typed at the top of some copies of a card; and then the not inconsiderable process of filing the cards into their correct places in the library's catalogues has to be carried out. The process of filing cards offers particular problems, especially if several copies of each catalogue are maintained, and the position can very quickly arise where the various catalogues and the various copies of catalogues are no longer maintained in step with one another. As a result the use of centrally prepared catalogue cards has been fairly restricted in Great Britain, and even where these cards have been used there has been considerable restriction to the types of catalogue and to the number of copies of catalogues that are maintained in a library.

The basis for the use of catalogue cards has been that the records on the cards contain most of the information needed by a library for the production of its catalogues. The same basis is equally true of machine readable records, but these records offer a far greater facility for the manipulation and modification of the information, and this should imply greater usefulness and greater economy in this processing work.

The Library of Congress in Washington set up towards the end of 1966 an experimental project with the title Project MARC to deal with the problems of creating and distributing machine readable catalogue records, and to give some libraries the opportunity to experiment in the use of such records for a number of purposes, the most significant of which was the production of a local catalogue records. United States libraries are completely accustomed to the local use of Library of Congress catalogue cards, in the form of a unit card with a main heading together with a list of additional author, title and subject headings, so that it was not surprising that the MARC records were designed particularly for the local production of Library of Congress cards.

Under Project MARC a number of libraries in the United States and the University Library of Toronto are receiving from the Library of Congress a weekly updated magnetic tape containing records with very full information for the majority of currently published English language monographs – there are at present about 800 new records each week. The Library of Congress is considering an extension of the project by the middle of the year to include records for an increasing number of foreign books and to make the tapes available to a greater number of libraries.

The aim of the Bodleian experiment with MARC tapes is to make use of the MARC records for the production of catalogue entries for a number of libraries, extending the present range of catalogues in these libraries.

Initially the experiment will be restricted to the Bodleian libraries (The Bodleian, Radcliffe Science Library, Rhodes House, the Law Library and the Indian Institute), where normally only one copy of a book is acquired for the whole Bodleian complex; when the procedures for this stage are established the experiment will be extended to other Oxford libraries to establish procedures for dealing with multiple copies of the same book acquired at different times. The experiment is not at this stage concerned with acquisition records.

The processes to be carried out are briefly as follows:–

1 To find weekly when there is a match between the currently published British and American books received at the Bodleian libraries and the records on the MARC file.

2 To print out the results of the search in a way that makes it easily possible for cataloguers to examine a printed out record alongside the corresponding book.

3 To decide on the modifications and additions to a MARC record that are necessary to create a master Bodleian record.

4 To print catalogues from the master file of Bodleian records for all the Bodleian libraries.

The situation in which the experiment is to be carried out is a rapidly changing one: firstly, the British National Bibliography is making preparations for the production of a British tape, containing records for all British publications, and this development will lead to a much closer concurrence of the acquisition of British books and the availability of the corresponding records, with records for almost all British books – in contrast to the situation with the Library of Congress MARC records where there are records for little over half of the British books published, with considerable delay in the availability of the majority of even these records;

THE MARC PROJECT RECORD
MARK DIAGNOSTIC LISTING

RECORD BATCH NO.   66-077791
CM00129

TYPE OF ENTRY(1) PERSONAL AUTHOR	FORM OF WORK(2) MONOGRAPH	BIBLIO(3) YES	ILLUS(4) YES	MAPS(5) NO	SUPPLEMENT NUMBER(6) NO	CONFERENCE OR MEETING(7) NO	JUVENILE WORK(8) NO	RECORD INDICATOR(9) NEW THIS WK

LANGUAGE DATA

CLASS(10) SINGLE	LANG 1(11) ENG	LANG 2(12)

PUBLICATION DATA

KEY(13) SINGLE	DATE 1(14) 1966	DATE 2(15)	PLACE(16) ENLO	NAME(17) BAJ	HEIGHT(18) 26 CM

TYPE OF SECONDARY ENTRY--------GS   SERIES-NO   LENGTH OF RECORD-0460
VARIABLE FIELDS-

L. C. CALL NUMBER	90	DA687.W5C3 1966a
DEWEY CLASS. NUMBER	92	283.4213
MAIN ENTRY	10	Carpenter, Edward Frederick.# 1910#- ed.
TITLE STATEMENT	20	A house of kings;# the history of Westminster Abbey,# edited by Edward Carpenter.
IMPRINT STATEMENT	30	London,# Baker.# 1966.# -/70/-
COLLATION STATEMENT	40	xix, 491 p. col. front., 66 plates (incl. 2 col.) tables, 25 1/2 cm.
NOTES	60	Bibliography: p. 465-471.
SUBJECT TRACING	70	Westminster Abbey.
TITLE TRACING	74	T
NATL. BIBLIO. NUMBER	830	(B66-12327)

secondly, the introduction of a Standard Book Number in 1968, with a unique number printed in a book, giving a means of matching records with books comparable to that of the Library of Congress Card Number system that exists already for American books.

MAIN TRENDS OF MECHANIZATION AND AUTOMATION OF SCIENTIFIC AND TECHNICAL INFORMATION IN CZECHOSLOVAKIA

JAROSLAV DORSKY

COSTEI, Prague

Early work began with edge-pinched and Peek-a-boo cards, but the foundation of COSTEI in 1965 led to more attention to the role of punched card machines and computers. The Department of Theoretical Research investigates basic theory, users' needs, processing methods and mathematcal models of information systems. The Department of Experimental Research deals with applications of all technologies, including computers and reprographic equipment. It will set up a laboratory for making and testing prototypes and new machines. The Methodological Department covers standards, professional training, information about information, and professional publications. The Section of Research Co-ordination co-ordinates basic research programmes and international co-operation. COSTEI itself functions as the national centre for research and development of scientific and technical information systems and services in all fields.

In the first phase computers are to be introduced into practical use, while transmission routes are to be solved under the present organizational conditions adapted to the information methodology. The aim of the first phase will be to assess, using available means;
- individual current awareness service for information users about the latest achievements in their branch
- answering enquiries concerning special problems in the form of keywords
- information retrieval
- systematic relatively complete new data surveys in form of indexes
- materials for scientific management of the information system

The second phase solves and creates conditions for qualitative changes of the information process on the basis of exact theoretical research.

The mechanization of the Czech information system is divided into three stages.

The aim of the first period is mechanized operation of information holdings of COSTEI, elaboration of model mechanization project for small and medium size information holdings, securing of pre-conditions for building up of a computer unit as COSTEI equipped with the latest means of computer technique and, finally, the elaboration and materialization of a professional training system for automated operation.

In the second period the setting-up of a modern computer unit is to be accomplished, mechanized processing of the information sources of COSTEI extended to disciplinary information centres with the aim to gradually establish an integrated, mechanized, nation-wide information system; moreover, in the course of the second period the possibilities of international co-operation, particularly as concerns the exchange of mechanically processed (computerized) records should be practically tested.

The third period should involve completion of mechanization of all keypoints of the Czechoslovak STEI system so as to secure its fully mechanized or partially automated operation; simultaneously, its linking up with the international information system is suggested.

The research programme has six main tasks:

1 Theory of scientific information
2 System and specialization of scientific and professional libraries
3 Classification of information
4 Methods of information processing
5 Investigation into mechanized systems of information storage, retrieval and distribution
6 Dissemination of knowledge, education, training and professional literature in the field of STEI

Special research tasks are to deal with systems in chemical structure data, radiation hygiene, electrical engineering, patents, and library housekeeping. (See the papers by A. Merta and J. Helbich.)

Mechanization projects within COSTEI, of primary and secondary holdings, began with the record of translations, using an IBM 1401; this will develop into an automated central record, and is being assessed using the DATA SAAB D21 computer. A second task is the mechanization of systems in the State Technical Library. A third studies the Automated Documentation and Information System (ARDIS), originally planned for a National-Elliott 803B computer and now being transferred to the more economically effective MINSK 222. A training course in the system MINSK-ARDIS began in 1967.

By the end of 1969 we also want to solve the methods of co-operation with scientific libraries, in particular with respect to suitable unification of working methods and organization principles. In the field of secondary holdings, mechanized central recording of scientific research and development work is already operating using Czechoslovak alphanumeric 90 column punched-card machines ARITMA. Information sorting is performed on the basis of descriptors, the 5-figure numeric descriptor consisting of the catchwords of the original information. From the individual catchwords a thesaurus is created during the operation of the system; the thesaurus is revised at 1 year periods so as to make it available for all information workers of our scientific and research basis.

According to the content of the information entry the information processing centre makes out two or three types of punched cards, viz.:

1 Descriptor or information punched cards containing, besides the current number of the entry, number of descriptors (sometimes overreaching the capacity of the card) and current number of the punched card, a 5-column searching field for 5-figure numeric descriptor of the categorized concept. Through the searching field all descriptors will subsequently pass and thus their number represents at the same time the number of punched cards of this sort. The descriptor punched card further contains 11 fixed fields for the arbitrarily located remaining 5-figure descriptors, always arranged in the same way as in the original material and the first punched card.

2 Thematic relation cards in which formal data are punched; they also contain a 3-column searching field through which all thematic relations will subsequently pass, in the same way as the descriptors in the searching field of the descriptor punched cards, as well as fixed 3-column fields for arbitrarily located three-figure thematic relations (the maximum number being 7).

3 Supplementary descriptor punched cards, used only if the information entry contains more than 11 catchwords, which is the maximum number that can be punched on one descriptor punched card.

The paper presents an outline of the plans for mechanization and automation of STEI in Czechoslovakia. The present review implies that we are faced with numerous exacting and difficult tasks. Yet it is worth noticing, and I am glad to emphasize the fact, that in our country material and personal preconditions are gradually created to provide for successful solutions of these problems and that their social import is acknowledged by including them into the state plan of development of science and technology, which comprises the staple tasks of our research and development. This is without doubt a very important step forward for estimation of the role of information activity in our country.

RESEARCH TOWARDS A COMPREHENSIVE COMPUTER-BASED INFORMATION SERVICE

T. M. AITCHISON

Institution of Electrical Engineers, London

The Institution of Electrical Engineers has, since 1898, been responsible for publishing the major English-language abstracts journals covering
the fields of physics and electrical engineering. Since that time, developments in these fields have resulted in a steady growth in the number of
articles abstracted by the two original publications and in the appearance
of a third abstracts journal to cover the rapidly growing field of control
engineering. Recently, too, the need for a quick, cheap means of informing scientists and engineers of recently published articles has become apparent and has been supplied by means of the 'Current Papers' series of
publications.

Thus, today, the Institution's INSPEC organisation (Information
Service in Physics, Electrotechnology and Control) publishes three abstracts journals (which, between them, are expected this year to include
75,000 abstracts):

> Physics Abstracts
> Electrical & Electronics Abstracts
> and Control Abstracts

together with the associated current-awareness publications

> Current Papers in Physics
> Current Papers in Electrotechnology
> and Current Papers on Control

Both in these publications, and in the research and development work
on which I propose to touch briefly in this paper, the Institution of
Electrical Engineers has the support of the leading American as well as
British learned societies in the fields covered by INSPEC.
These are

> the American Institute of Physics (U.S.)
> the Institute of Physics and the Physical Society (U.K.)
> the Institute of Electrical & Electronics Engineers (U.S.)
> and the Institution of Electronic & Radio Engineers (U.K.)

At present the INSPEC publications are produced conventionally but
work is in hand to mechanize their production. It is planned to produce a
machine-readable file of unit records. By computer manipulation of this

file and photo-typesetting the present INSPEC abstracts journals and current-awareness publications will be produced, as well as the indexes to the abstract journals in whatever cumulations are desired.

All the data required to produce this series of publications and their indexes will be selected by a once-for-all intellectual effort and transferred to machine-readable form by a single keyboarding operation. In addition to this use for the mechanized production of the present series of publications, it is planned to extend the range of INSPEC services using the same machine file of unit records. Among the new services envisaged are the selective dissemination of information, facilities for retrospective searching, and the supply of copies of the unit-record file in machine-readable form.

This mechanisation and expansion of INSPEC requires an extensive research and development programme. Rather than merely catalogue all the various projects included in the programme I feel it would be more useful and, I hope, interesting if I were to concentrate for a few minutes each on two of the projects. One, the S.D.I. Investigation, is being conducted in support of the expansion objective; the other, the comparative evaluation of indexing languages, is related to both the mechanization of the current publications and the expansion of services.

S.D.I. INVESTIGATION

The S.D.I. Investigation is designed to assess the value, economics, efficiency and acceptability to user of the Selective Dissemination of Information or S.D.I. system.

To do this an S.D.I. system will be established to serve some 600 research workers in electronics, providing them with an experimental service for six months and an operational service for one year. In return for this weekly S.D.I. service, which they will receive free of charge, the 600 research workers or 'users' will be expected to provide weekly assessments of the service and provide other information as required.

The research workers will be a random selection from government research establishments, industry and universities and colleges of technology. They will receive notifications of English-language periodical articles in the field of electronics research: it is expected that these will number some 240 items per week.

The index language used will be a development by the Institution of Electrical Engineers of the Thesaurus of Engineering Terms of the Engineers' Joint Council of the U.S. The indexing will use neither links, roles nor weighting, that is the descriptors or keywords or key-phrases will merely be listed for each paper with no attempt to associate them, show their relationship, or assess their relative value.

The user-profiles, that is the description of the subject interests of the individual research worker, will, on the other hand, show the relationship of the terms by a simple Boolean logic expression.

The main feedback required from each user (so that adjustments may be made to his profile to ensure that his requirements are more and more nearly satisfied) consists of the weekly relevance assessments of the notifications sent to him. This allows the Precision figure to be calculated.

To obtain an equivalent figure for Recall (or how many notifications were not sent which should have been) each user will receive periodically a print-out of the week's total accessions and be asked to mark those he considers relevant. These will then be compared with his S.D.I. notifications for the week. The notifications will not, of course, be supplied to him until the marking of the print-out has been completed.

The assessment of the value, usefulness and acceptability of the S.D.I. service by the users must, of necessity, be subjective but these judgements will be supplemented by more objective measurements such as the rate of withdrawal from the service, the number of notified documents which the user sought to obtain, and what proportion of papers found most useful were notified in the S.D.I. service.

In the course of the project a number of other investigations will be made. These will include the acceptability of different formats, (i.e. unit cards or listings) and of types of notifications, i.e. whether titles alone, titles with lists of descriptors, or titles with abstracts are most valuable for assessing the relevance of documents and which are preferred.

However the investigation which is of equal importance to the survey of value, usefulness and acceptability of the S.D.I. service is the measurement of change in information-gathering habits. Since S.D.I. is a new current-awareness dissemination system it will be of interest and value to discover what changes, if any, it produces in the information-gathering habits of users and in their general approach to information. The results of recent surveys of scientists' approach to information are sufficiently serious to make it desirable to find out whether the present situation is capable of being changed to a more rational pattern.

To investigate any change in information-gathering habits, the user group will be surveyed by questionnaire before the start of the S.D.I. service and the survey will be repeated when they have been receiving the service as a routine for at least a year. To evaluate the contribution of any other factors to the changes found, a control group of research workers who will not receive the S.D.I. service will be surveyed similarly on both occasions. Also, to assess the proportion of the change which may be due to the regular receipt of a current-awareness service rather than specifically to S.D.I., half the members of the control group will be provided during the period of the S.D.I. service with copies of either *Current Papers in Physics* or *Current Papers in Electrotechnology*.

Throughout the S.D.I. Investigation much will depend on the co-operation of the librarians and information officers in the users' organisations. We have high hopes that this assistance will be forthcoming since we have already received a quite remarkable degree of very willing co-operation in the earlier phases of the project.

However, before we leave the S.D.I. Investigation one point must be emphasized. The investigation is concerned with the total system and its interaction with the user: it does not seek to develop a particular method of indexing, profile compilation or up-dating, or computer manipulation. Thus no attempt will be made to compare the performance of different index languages as part of the S.D.I. Investigation nor to seek the maximum mechanization of the system, for example by automatic indexing or automatic compilation or up-dating of profiles.

COMPARATIVE EVALUATION OF INDEXING LANGUAGES

It has already been mentioned that for the S.D.I. Investigation post-coordinate indexing using an index language of the E.J.C. type will be used.This was chosen for the Investigation after preliminary trials had confirmed its suitability.

However, it does not follow that the same index language will be used for the regular S.D.I. service which will subsequently be provided as part of INSPEC. It is hoped that for the complete range of services eventually established only one indexing operation and, essentially, one index language will be required. Thus the language chosen must be suitable for the printed indexes to the abstracts journals, and searches of the machine file, as well as S.D.I.

Initially it is proposed to evaluate the various possible languages on the basis of their use for retrieval in the machine file. When this evaluation has been completed the relationship of the index languages to the printed index, their use in the S.D.I. system, and their relationship to other aspects of INSPEC will be considered.

In all, six index languages will be investigated. To avoid confusion perhaps it should be explained that "index language" is being used hereto include not only added index terms but also the words of the title or abstract when used for retrieval.

The languages to be investigated are:

1 Terms in the title of the paper, erport, etc.
2 Terms in the abstracts, i.e. similar to (1) but of greater exhaustivity.
3 Science Abstracts subject headings with modifier line. This is the system used at present for the printed indexes to the abstracts journals. The subject heading is a controlled language whereas the words of the modifier line, a modification of the title where required to make it more informative, are uncontrolled.
4 Selected natural-language, single terms, i.e. single terms selected by indexers as indicating the subject content of the document, with complete freedom of choice in synonyms, etc.
5 Descriptors used in the S.D.I. Investigation.
6 A specially-developed controlled, faceted language, which it is hoped will be available from our U.S. associates.

Each of these languages has its own claim to adoption. For example, the first two require no indexing of input and the third requires no additional indexing since it is generated for the printed index. Again the sixth may be used in the indexing of a group of primary journals which represent a substantial percentage of the input to INSPEC and which will, at a later stage, be available in machine-readable form.

In this index-language evaluation, use will be made of the material and facilities of the S.D.I. Investigation. The test collection of documents will be selected from the document collection used for the initial matching test of the S.D.I. Investigation and the test questions will be obtained from S.D.I. users. Also, for two of the languages to be evaluated, the indexing of the documents used in the evaluation will be that carried out in the S.D.I. Investigation.

Working in conjunction with the S.D.I. Investigation will also provide an opportunity to obtain a more accurate measure of recall. In the usual method of obtaining a measure of recall, all of the documents in the collection must be assessed for relevance to each question. If the collection contains more than 30 or 40 documents it is difficult to persuade an enquirer to undertake the assessment or to carry it out consistently. In this index-language evaluation questions would be invited within the subject area of the questioner's profile. Thus only those documents which had already been assessed as relevant to a profile need be considered for relevance to the question provided by the owner of the profile.

One hundred questions relating to profiles which have had an acceptable number of documents assessed as relevant to them will be selected and a test collection of at least 500 documents assembled from the documents relevant to these profiles.

A machine file of the questions translated into the index languages and the documents indexed by these languages will be set up and a total of 20 searches made to include various combinations of question and document indexing.

As recently as last year, the majority of information workers would have had no doubt that a vocabulary such as the S.D.I. descriptors or the faceted classification would prove much superior to the others. It was believed that the intellectual effort required for the design of a structured index language and for its application in indexing must bring rewards in improved performance.

However Cleverdon's results in the 2nd Aslib Cranfield Project appear to show that the long-held views on the disadvantages of natural-language and the superiority of controlled and structured languages may have to be revised.

At present his findings are too unexpected and disturbing for us to accept them immediately but they are sufficiently convincing for us to feel that it is well worth while to include in the investigation those index languages such as titles, abstracts, or subject heading and modifier line which will be present in the machine file and require no extra indexing effort.

OTHER INVESTIGATIONS

There are a number of other investigations in hand, many of them concerned with the use of the present services and the potential interest in possible new services. The question of the optimum subject coverage of INSPEC has been under constant review but will be considered afresh in the present programme. Similarly the classes of material, for example technical reports, preprints of conference papers, patents, and trade literature, which should be included in INSPEC will be investigated at this time since mechanisation will greatly reduce the difficulties involved in a rapid expansion in the number of items covered.

This re-examination of the whole INSPEC system presents a most exciting challenge. We must look ahead to a situation where only a proportion of the information disseminated by INSPEC is in printed form; where much of it is distributed in machine-readable form to other organisation where it will be further processed to meet their individual requirements; and where the INSPEC file may be searched on-line from remote locations.

CENTRALIZED AND DECENTRALIZED ABSTRACTING AND INDEXING IN THE LIGHT OF CZECHOSLOVAK EXPERIENCE

JOSEF VORACEK

COSTEI, Prague

The early beginnings of information activities in the modern sense of the word are associated in Czechoslovakia with the name of the Masaryk Academy of Work and date back to 1926. The idea of information service was taken up later on by several large industrial concerns, the Skoda Works, the Brno Small Arms Factory and the Ceskomoravske Engineering Works among them. It was the library department of the Skoda Works that developed it to the most advanced level. Founded in 1930, it based its work on the use of the UDC, was selective in the sense that it selected sources of information in fields of engineering, and inside the establishment relied on the "addressed-to-individuals" mode of distribution.

The general, and let us say directly, the national significance of information activities was not recognized until much later. In 1944 there was founded at the Masaryk Academy of Work (renamed The Czech Academy of Technology during the war) a Committee of Documentation, followed in 1946 by a decree of the Ministry of Education instituting the founding of the Technical Documentation Centre as a department of the Technical Universities Library, now the State Technical Library. The activities that ensued there were based on the use of the UDC. After 1954 technical subjects were supplemented by subjects from the field of economics. Considering that the selection, processing and dissemination of information were done centrally from one place, we may well understand the reason why the whole of information work has taken on a somewhat encyclopaedic character and become a portrayal of an appreciable part of the system of contemporary knowledge, but the various scientific disciplines appearing in the Abstract of the UDC published in 1954 were not condensed uniformly enough. Thus the whole science of mathematics was reduced in the Abstract to 32 groups as against the 56 main groups and 639 subgroups used say by Mathematical Reviews, to quote an example. It thus came about that the calculus of probability and mathematical statistics were included in a single group (519.2) with the result that, as of today, this group, deposited in the card file of the Central Documentation Fund, contains over 1,600 abstracts; it goes without saying that searching for any concrete subject among this multitude is very laborious and time-consuming. To avoid this, it would be necessary, whenever so many abstracts have accumulated, to arrange them further according to some additional classification principle; by doing so we would, however, violate the unity of the classification system adopted, and make the principle of the Abstract open to doubt. The same situation exists in e.g. the group dealing with the capitalistic system of national economy (33B) in which about 3,000 cards have accumulated. Furthermore, the given time-conditioned principle must of necessity become obsolete as soon as new scientific disciplines come into being, or as soon as ever additional branches of science are drawn into or emphasized in engineering. The case in point in the first instance is nuclear physics and nuclear engineering which were added to the Abstract in the form of an appendix; in the second instance, today's emphasis on work psychology, sociometry and management, fields in which the shortcomings of the principle are plain to see even now.

In passing to the processing of an ever larger number of technical and scientific disciplines, the activities take on the character of a definite system strengthened mainly by the fact that both the processor and the disseminator are a single institution. This method of centralized processing of scientific disciplines within a closed system was, at the time the Czechoslovak system was being formed, already realized in two outstanding ways which, however, we have failed to follow. The method leads to the idea of making the information system a reflection of the system of sciences and of the whole of human knowledge. It is interesting to note that the idea was converted into fact in two countries, namely France and the Soviet Union. In France this has undoubtedly been supported by the strong tradition of positivism which has created a system of science classification based on principles well recognizable in the structure of the *Bulletin signalétique*. The classification used there is the well-known classification of sciences according to the order of decreasing generality elaborated by Comte, in the sequence mathematics, astronomy, physics, chemistry, biology and sociology. This is reflected in the *Bulletin signalétique* by the fact that the sections on mathematics, astronomy, physics and chemistry form the beginning, and those on social science, termed there "sciences humaines" the end of the chain. The objections against this principle of classification are quite familiar: mathematics should be preceded by logic which is common to all sciences and gaining in importance with the march of time. Apart from this, the relations between sciences are not as linear as assumed by positivism; this is also recognized by the other, similar system, the *Referativnyi Zhurnal.* French scientism comes also into play in section 9 covering engineering and called "Science de l'ingenieur", placed to follow applied chemistry, whose 16,000 titles per year make it equal to half the section 6 "Structure de la matière". The question of what to do with problems common to several scientific disciplines, or with the fact that one and the same problem may be considered from several aspects, has been solved by the *Bulletin signalétique* by *repeating* data on such problems in several sections and marking them in a special way.

The classification system of the *Referativnyi Zhurnal* is based on a system of sciences elaborated by Engels in the sequence mechanics, physics, chemistry, biology, with mathematics and biochemistry introduced ex post to form the series mathematics, mechanics, physics, chemistry biochemistry, biology. This is the system adopted for the Rubricator of the *Referativnyi Zhurnal*. The index used for designating the various scientific and engineering fields is arranged in Russian alphabet and starts with automation to which is assigned number 01. The numbering should not, of course, deceive us as to the true nature of the origin of this classification which unlike the French one, considers the relations between sciences to be complicated.

Nor has this system avoided the two pitfalls that represent the weakest spot of universal systems of this sort, viz. viewing a concrete theme from several aspects or repeating it in several disciplines. The *Referativnyi Zhurnal* has solved this problem by dividing the theme in several sections depending on the aspect being considered. Thus e.g. the concept of cavitation is assigned to section 16 B-mechanics, where it covers cavitation in the mechanical sense and cavitation in pumps; in section 21 D it refers to cavitation of hydraulic equipment and piping; in 05 A to cavitation of ship propellers. It also appears in section 18Z-physics of ultrasound. Liquids are found in section 18 B-physics of gases and liquids, and in 19 B-general problems of chemistry; non-Newtonian liquids are in section 16 B-hydromechanics; super-conductivity is dealt with in sections 18 E and 21 B, electron microscope in sections 18 A, 23 A, 19 D; magnetization in 18 E, 15 I and 21 A; industrial aesthetics is covered in seven sections according to the Rubricator, and in four sections according to the Index issued in 1966; plasticity in sections 16 B, 19 C and 15 D, etc. To restrict searching to the pertinent section one must either know or have defined the principle according to which the subject matter is classified in various sections of the *Referativnyi Zhurnal*. As such classification is often a thing of subjective viewpoint on the part of the processor, searching in this system is in every case a complicated affair.

The problems of economics and of social sciences in direct relation to manufacture are treated by the *Referativnyi Zhurnal* in a special section, Industrial economics. Using the Rubricator and setting up from this section a list of key concepts, we arrive at some 80 to 100 keywords including those used in a new section devoted to the organization of industrial management. We thus face the same shortcoming which we have noted as accompanying the use of the UDC; this means that this system, too, departs in the field in question from its main advantage, the advantage of completeness and of certain universality.

We have discussed so far two systems of centralized processing of information: one represented by the former Czechoslovak centralized processing of scientific and engineering fields using for classification principle the Abstract from the UDC. the other embodying that of the *Bulletin signalétique* and of the *Referativnyi Zhurnal* with classification based essentially on the logic of the sciences.

The third system is the decentralized system of information processing based on the classification principle of the Abstract from the UDC. This system has recently been realized in Czechoslovakia by decentralizing the processing and dissemination of information to branch information centres while leaving the Central Documentation Fund entrusted with the duty of selective filing. In this way the structure of the information system became a reflection of the organization of our industry, and as it was revealed later on, also of the contemporary scope of our production. The first consequence arising from the introduction of this system was multiple bibliographic processing of sources dealing with problems common to a number of industrial branches, such as those on automatic control, packaging couplings, etc. Thus in 1964 sources referring to automatic control were processed by 11 information departments, packaging engineering by 10, palletization by 16, journal bearings by 15, shafts by 15, couplings by 16, loading and unloading equipment by 25, and compressed air haulage by 22 departments. But worse than this drawback which in many cases led to multiple abstracting of one source, was the dearth of information from fields marginal to the engineering fields being followed. Let us by way of an example quote the case of cooling towers, in the group for which we found no abstracts from several journals such as British Plastics, Materials Protection, Concrete and Construction Engineering, Génie Civil; this we may take to signify that important data on the use of plastics and other unconventional structural materials have likely been omitted from the system. It soon became apparent from the way the abstracts were made that the information staff of industrial concerns is in the literary sphere often satisfied with a somewhat sketchy, general orientation. The problem could undoubtedly be solved by expedient coordination of efforts; this, however, is regarded in the light of the large number of people involved in the preparation of abstracts, as both costly and difficult to carry through. On the other hand the system possesses the advantage of serving the instantaneious needs of industry faster and more readily than the encyclopaedic system; this is, of course done, at the price that the completeness of information material will be found definitely inspired at the time the thematic interest will assume different configuration and call for more profound researches into other than the present-day topics. The fact that such changes in the sphere of interest are actually taking place has been observed all along in studies made continually at the Central Documentation Fund, and is acknowledged in the new Abstract from the UDC whose principles of condensation to some extent differ from those of the first one and thus clearly document the shifting interest (e.g. mathematics now has 83 main groups), discounting, of course, the expansion of the scientific and engineering fields contingent on new findings.

We have in this way exhausted the systems that attempt to record as completely as possible a defined field of science and technology. By its completeness, the French system answers well the conception of the unity of sciences and their development with a decreasing order of generality as we know them from logical disciplines; it does not, however, achieve the range represented by the *Referativnyi Zhurnal.* But this fundamental classification of sciences based on a logical principle, has not cleared itself of problems attached to the division of the subject matter inside the various sections, nor of the problem of delimiting the contents of the sections with respect to one another. Systems of this kind are successful whenever we wish to gain an overal view of a broader field in general; if, on the other hand, our interest is focused on a specific question the encyclopaedic systems are no longer as effective as index systems. If the references to the *Referativnyi Zhurnal* or to the *Bulletin signaletique* are to be really beneficial, we must know the whole system first.

This brings us to the last system whose realization is also being contemplated in Czechoslovakia, namely the processing of sources from scientific and technical fields by help of the index system. This method has been successfully applied in the English-speaking countries where it led e.g. to the *Engineering Index,* a review of world literature which our Central Documentation Fund finds to be the one most widely referred to (next to *Chemical Abstracts*) of all our information sources from abroad, and to the *British Technology Index* experiencing in our Central Documentation Fund its second year of increasing popularity. In the Engineering Index the bibliographic data are supplemented by brief abstracts, in the *British Technology Index*, the contents of the documents are given by its exact classification under the pertinent term of the indexing or descriptor language, with a one-to-one correlation between concept and symbol. The advantage of this latter system lies unquestionably in that it permits rapid orientation in retrospective searching, since the arrangement of the terms is alphabetical and the descriptor language pays due respect to relations between things on the one side and their contingent Properties, Actions and Parts on the other. The order of the verbal elements is that of diminishing concreteness, the most concrete term forming the entry word. The interval between the published paper and the appearance of its entry is also very short. I am of the opinion that indexing would be a very convenient method or processing Czechoslovak scientific and engineering literature. A vocabulary serving the needs of indexing would be free of the common lexical language which maintains for the most part the features of the natural language. But so far as the processing of all, i.e. the world's, technical and scientific literature is concerned, the method is not to be recommended at the present state of the art because of certain peculiarities of the Czech language which I shall mention in the next paragraphs.

The predominant proportion of world technical and scientific literature is written in English. The Czech formation of words and hence also of professional terms differs essentially from the English one. There would be no special difficulties experienced in the formation of Czech expressions equivalent to what is called "single terms" in English. Such cases, however, occur exceedingly seldom, i.e. when we are dealing with an object with no alternatives, or when the terms in question are entirely new and thus also unique, or finally, when the terms are isolated by their meaning and without relation.

Most professional terms are compound, however. In Czech such terms are likely to consist of nouns and adjectives, or of two nouns the second of which is in the genitive case or in the pre-position form. It should be realized, at the same time, that adjectives denote quality or state, with the quality referring mostly to a large number of subjects, as is the case when it denotes colours, dimensions, substance properties, etc. This is the reason why in Czech, just as in Russian, the indexes are formed of nouns. The sole exception to this rule is, to the best of my knowledge, the section on chemistry in the *Referativnyi Zhurnal* where the index employs adjectives (e.g. "Koksovyi gaz"—town gas, "lignosulfonovyie kisloty"—lignosulphonic acids); but this method is restricted to the relatively narrow field of chemistry and could not consistently be applied in Czech, where, in addition, the ending of the adjective in chemistry simultaneously determines the valency. The circumstances which I have just noted pose problems that are hard to master in the setting up of an index in the Czech language.

Let us take by way of an example the Czech term for the electron beam—**elektronovy** paprsek. Paprsek is here a noun, elektronový an adjective. Classifying the expression under the term "paprsek", the word will appear in a polytechnical index within a group containing altogether 54 different kinds of paprsek, such as svetelný paprsek—luminous ray, paprsek páry—steam jet, not mentioning paprsek kola whose English equivalent is wheel spoke. By such a lexical classification we completely lose the factual connection between concepts.

As another example let us use the expression "tepelná úprava" whose English equivalent is heat treatment; the word úprava is a noun, tepelná an adjective. If classified under the word "úprava", the expression will appear in a group of a total of 43 different "úprava", with no connection whatsoever between them as evidence by the following:

úprava suchá — dry concentration
úprava typographická — typographic arrangement
úprava usni — dressing process
úprava krajiny — landscape design, etc.

Here again the factual connection is completely lost and degenerated to a lexical connection

The third example deals with the expression fluidni vrstva-fluidized bed in English. Vrstva is a noun, fluidni an adjective. Classifying the expression under the word "vrstva" we shall get it in connection with 82 concepts whose heterogeneity is quite evident from a few chosen at random for the

purposes of illustration:
    Vrstva adhesivni – tie gum
    vrstva kryci – floor finish
    vrstva zákalná – hardening zone
    vrstva vzduchová – air space
    vrstva tenká – thin film, etc.
As an example of an expression compounded of two nouns I shall mention bod varu—boiling point. The first of the two nouns is the subject, the second denotes a state and is in the genitive case. In a polytechnical index the expression classified under the term "bod" would appear in a group of 153 concepts such as:
    bod dělící – point of division
    bod kritický – transition point
    bod modulový – modular point
    bod nasycení – saturation point, etc.
Were we to consistently observe in the classification the peculiarities of the Czech language, we should arrive at an acumulation of material under general concepts whose singularities are expressed by an adjective or by the genitive case. Were we, on the other hand, to classify the expressions under superior concepts and observe the principle of factual connection, we would violate the principle of alphabetical arrangement, the cornerstone of rapid orientation, and thus excessively enlarge the cross-reference system, the extent of disadvantages being in proportion to the degree of generality.

The situation would in no way be different were we to use the adjective forms. In the lexical practice, the latter have been used in e.g. the *Czech Technical Encyclopaedia.* As I have already pointed out, the adjective forms express the shape, dimensional, substance, functional, etc. properties which are apt to apply to a whole series of subjects. In using them we would essentially replace a fairly broad index term by a heading with at least equal generality while weakening the natural emphasis which the Czech language puts on nouns. An analysis of a few cases recorded in the *Czech Technical Encyclopaedia* will convince us that the use of adjective froms in the elaboration of an index is a highly intricate problem. It is quite clear from the above that Czech scientific terms were not created or formed with a view to these needs. Another difficulty will arise owing to the necessity of applying the fundamental princples that underlie the setting up of an index, consistently to all fields, to make known in advance the precepts that govern the use of the index, irrespective of whe ther or not this is in harmony with the way of thinking in a particular, narrower, field.

Difficulties are also likely to be experienced in the endeavour to class· ify concepts according to diminishing concreteness which is very hard to determine because of the development of the language towards abstractness.

In view of all I have said so far, I should like to recommend to apply first the index system to the processing of Czech and Slovak scientific and technical literature. In collaboration with experts and institutions exercising an influence on the formation of professional language we shall be in a position to purify certain expressions, bring them in better correlation with the concepts and in clearer factual connections than they are at the present time when professional terminology is predominantly lexical. It will also be necessary to pay due regard to the needs of technical language when preparing engineering standards with their compulsory terms.

It is my opinion that the information activities in Czechoslovakia will continue for some time to come to be carried on in the decentralized system using the Abstract of the UDC. The system will certainly be improved by coordination of effort. The primary task that awaits us in the next stage is to set up an index whose successful elaboration is a sine qua non for any higher type of information services.

Surveying now the development up till now of information activities in Czechoslovakia we feel compelled to admit that the choice of centralized processing in the form of abstracts has indeed been a very expedient initial solution. This system ensured us of long term stability, and any changes that arose were produced solely by changes in the sphere of interest, since in such cases the scope of processed material was no longer covered by the condensed classification system used. This stability offered us plenty of time in which to try out new solutions. But I do not think that this time has been exploited effectively enough.

INDORES 4 – A MECHANIZED SYSTEM OF INFORMATION RETRIEVAL IN THE FIELD OF INFORMATION SCIENCE

AUGUSTIN MERTA

*Centre for Inventions and Scientific Information,
Czechoslovak Academy of Sciences. Prague.*

Project INDORES 4 is a part of comparative research-project INDORES which has been carried out in the Centre for Inventions and Scientific Information (CISI) of the Czechoslovak Academy of Sciences, since 1965. This centre methodologically directs activity of scientific information departments in more than one hundred institutes of natural, technical and social sciences of the Academy. CISI is trying to build up a coordinated network of the Academy's scientific information (SI) centres. Special attention is given to the problem of computerized processing of SI.

Within the framework of its research into methodological problems of SI, CISI began to experiment in the field of mechanization of storing and retrieving of SI. Experience gained is fully exploited by CISI during consultations in SI departments of academic institutes.

Therefore CISI began in 1965 the experimental project INDORES which is the comparative study of four mechanized SI processing methods, using the same store of documents and the identical indexing system. The compared systems are: peek-a-boo cards (INDORES), edgepunched cards (INDORES 2), punched cards machine (INDORES 3) and computerized system of SI (INDORES 4). The whole research has not yet been finished, but the results and experience cleared up the causes of decline of edge-punched cards and punched-cards machines methods and increase of peek-a-boo cards in personal documentation systems, and of computer methods in big institutional or integrated SI systems.

In this paper we shall speak only about the computerized project INDORES 4.

PRINCIPLES OF PROJECT INDORES 4

INDORES 4 is a universally applicable computerized SI system, using the Czechoslovak computer EPOS 2. It is a medium-size computer with a ferrit-internal memory of 10,000 characters capacity. Two magnetic drum memories within the capacity of 10,000 characters or magnetic tapes create external memories. EPOS is designed with time-sharing working possibility. Input is possible by punched cards, punched tapes or teletypes. Output unit is represented by a 120 characters printer. As one can see, this computer is not suitable for a large operating SI system. For a pilot-size experiment INDORES, computer EPOS is large enough, CISI is preparing reprogramming the project for a big IBM 7040 computer in 1968–69. Project INDORES 4 is based on these principles:

1 The whole programme contains 4 subprogrammes of storing, retrieving, disseminating of SI and preparing author or subject indexes by computer.

2 Experimentally, the literature dealing with information science and techniques has been processed. Project supposes application in any part of science.

3 Classification system used, is of faceted character with nemonic, alphanumeric notation (full details in ref. 1). Maximum 9 descriptors may be used for one document. Originally 12 descriptors could be used. But after statistical investigation has shown that only 2% of documents were indexed with more than 9 descriptors, we have reduced it, to save the capacity of computor's internal memory. When reprogramming the project for a bigger computer, we shall again raise the number of indexes to fulfil the condition of depth analysis and indexing.

Faceted classification proved to be successful, because no rôle-indicators have to be included in the classification formula. Link indicators are necessary, unless we do not decide to prepare two or more appropriate entries for one document. Generally, indexes have the firm, four-level hierarchical formula.

4 The input is with 90 column punched cards Aritma of Czechoslovak origin. Conversion for punched tapes is possible. For one document 5 cards are being punched. The punched cards enable us to do, quite easily and cheaply, the necessary statistical investigations when preparing an appropriate thesaurus or classification scheme.

5 Project is using the special alphanumeric code EPOS. This code includes letters of all latin-based alphabets, arabic numerals and a suffucent store of marks for expressing logical relations in the retrieval formula. Using this code, the problem of transliteration is solved (except cyrilics and oriental script systems). For this purpose, a special accomodation of standard card-punch-machine was necessary.

6 Search questions are introduced into the computer by punched cards or by tape in the code of natural language. The search-formula in the notation of the indexing language is added. The logical relations between individual key-words of questions are expressed by Boolean algebra symbols of conjunction, disjunction, negation or their combinations. The sample of a question formula is in fig. 4. Input of conjunction and negation operations is done by one punched-card. Disjunctive questions need as many entries as there are components included in the search formula. The control of relevance-ratio is carried out by devising several different search formulas for the same question and comparing re-

sults, obtained after using them all. If the result of a search is negative (no relevant sources found), programme of searching to hierarchically higher index is, if necessary, introduced.

7   Computer answers simultaneously several questions (up to the maximum of 35). After reprogramming for a bigger computer, the number of questions can be two or three times higher. It is important for large SI systems, as well as for programmes of selective dissemination of SI. The time-sharing device enables simultaneous work on several different programmes.

8   Output is possible in several variations: through the computer-printer, teletype machine, phototype machine etc. According to the quantity of information, answers may have the form of:

accession numbers of relevant sources (in this case an accession-number-file must be on hand)
authors' index (programme is about to be finished)
full bibliographic data in every individual subject search
system of periodical answers to permanent questions (a selective dissemination system
different indexes (e.g. KWIC, KWOC, WADEX index etc; which will will be programmed in 1968–1969)

At the end of every group of simultaneously answered questions, computer prints: how many questions were answered, how many documents were searched through, how many of them were relevant at least to one question, and the amount of collation operations which had to be made. For experimental purposes these data are quite useful.

9   In the future all kinds of indexes will be produced from the basic bibliographic data-file. This planned in 1968–69 after coming over to a big computer. As the basic programmes for these purposes were solved in some Czechoslovak SI centres, reprogramming will bring technical rather than intellectual problems.

CONCLUSIONS

Experiences with our project INDORES have proved, in agreement with other projects of computerized SI systems developed in other countries, that in reality the differences between separate programmes for storing, retrieving and disseminating of SI, are rather small. They are given by the capacity of computer, as well as education and spirit of designer and programmer of appropriate SI project.

I think the time has come when we must consider seriously the international standardization of all basic programmes for storing, retrieving and disseminating of information. At the same time, all programmes should be created from the point of view of compatibility to different types of computers used in different countries. Standardization needs to be applied to the whole area of "Software" too. The most important seems to be creating international selecting languages for separate spheres of science and technology as well as for the whole social activity of mankind.

LITERATURE:

1   MERTA, A. – TOMAN, J.: "Sistema koordinatnogo indeksirovanija dlja obrabotki informacii s pomośĉju superpozicionnych perfokart s mnemotechniĉeskoj mnogorazmêrnoj notacijej" (A system of coordinated indexing using faceted classification with mnemonic alphanumoric notation). In the Proceedings of the Conference of Mechanized Information Systems, held in Moscow in 1965, pp. 258–271 (Kempleksnaja mechanizacija i avtomatizacia processov obrabetki, poiska, vykaĉi i peredaĉi na razstorjanije nauĉno-techniĉeskoj informacii, Trudy simpeziuma, 1966, Moskva, VINITI) (in Russian)
2   MERTA, A. – TOMAN, J.: "Projekt INDORES–srovnání ĉtyř metod mechanické selekce". (Project INDORES–the comparison of four methods of mechanized retrieval). Metodika a technika informací, 1967, No. 4. (in Czech).

DIRECT SELECTION OF KEYWORDS FOR THE KWIC INDEX

JAN HELBICH

Institute of Radiation Hygiene, Prague

Since 1965 the Institute of Radiation Hygiene has been publishing
the bibliographical journal *Index radiohygienicus* comprising current
world literature from the field of radiation hygiene and radiobiology.
In 10 issues provided with author and KWIC (semiannually cumul-
ated) indexes more than 6,000 bibliographical units are processed per
year. The programmes for the MINSK-22 computer were written by
Mr. E. Tschernoster from the Research Institute for Medical
Electronics and Modelling in Prague.

The KWIC index method suffers from three main drawbacks,
namely
1 the dependence on the adequacy of the titles alone as the source
of subject content clues
2 the uncontrolled vocabulary
3 the difficulties in performing combinations of keywords.

These, as well as other disadvantages are well known and some
ways of eliminating them have been suggested (1). The present communication will deal exclusively with the problem of keyword selection.

The author of the KWIC index method, H. P. LUHN, studied in
connection with automatic creation of literature abstracts (2) the relation between the frequency of words in the text and the resolving
power of keywords. It would seem tempting to use this relation also
for determining the keywords from the set of words contained in the
titles of publications for which we want to process the KWIC index.
Yet, already a simple analysis of a particular title set, e.g. of one volume of the journal *Health Physics,* shows that the occurrence is no
reliable indicator of the selective value of individual words. Table 1
demonstrates in 31 most frequent words that words of various selective value are mixed up, so that no demarcation line can be drawn
between the keywords and non-significant words when arranged
according to decreasing occurrence. This can't be changed even by the
fact that with decreasing occurrence the increasing prevalence of keywords over non-significant words is clearly manifest. (Table 2). The

keywords must be therefore determined in a different manner than by means of a simple occurrence analysis.

Table 1. Most frequent words from the titles of all articles in *Health Physics,* vol. 11 (1965)

COMMON WORDS		TERMS		SELECTIVE VALUE
OF	142			
THE	79			
AND	69			
IN	64			
A	32			
		RADIATION	25	−
ON	22			
TO	18	GAMMA	18	+
FOR	15			
BY	13			
		RADIONUCLIDE	12	−
FROM	10	DISTRIBUTION	10	+
		FALLOUT	10	++
		RETENTION	10	+
WITH	9	CESIUM−137	9	++
		ENVIRONMENTAL	9	+
		HEALTH	9	+
		RADIOACTIVE	9	−
HIGH	8			
AN	7	NATURAL	7	+
		RADIOACTIVITY	7	−
EFFECTS	6	BODY	6	+
		DETERMINATION	6	−
		DOSIMETRY	6	+
		NEUTRON	6	++
		RAY	6	

Table 2. Ratio (keywords/non-significant words) in titles from *Health Physics,* vol. 11 (1965).

OCCURRENCE	WORD TYPES	KEYWORDS	NON−SIG.WORDS	RATIO/KN
>1%	9	1	8	0,1
0,4−1%	16	8	8	1
<0.4%	625	417	208	2

In order to achieve the highest possible degree of automation of the indexing LUHN chose (3) an ingenious method of indirect keyword selection consisting in processing by the computer the text of the titles against a stop list of non-significant words to eliminate them from indexing. Nearly all known applications of the KWIC system employ the above indirect method; this obviously does not mean that there are no problems involved which would not require a more detailed study (4).

STOPLIST NO. EXTENT	CHEMICAL TITLES NO.	TITLES (THOUSANDS)	KEYWORDS (THOUSANDS)	KEYWORDS PER TITLE
1. 750	—	—	—	—
2. 950	EXP 2/1960	2·3	11·7	5·1
3. 439	1/1961	2·5	14·3	5·7
4. 360	13/1961	3·8	23·7	6·2
5. 330	15/1961	3·1	19·2	6·2
6. 328	1/1962	2·3	14·8	6·4
7. 306	11/1962	4·6	28·2	6·1
8. 1153	1/1963	3·1	18·7	6·0
9. 1295	16/1963	2·9	17·5	6·0
10. 1319	12/1965	3·7	21·4	5·8
11. 1337	5/1966	4·4	25·2	5·7

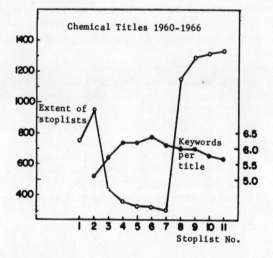

Table 3. and Fig. 1. Extent of individual stoplists of *Chemical Titles* 1960-1966 and average number of keywords per title in respective issues.

There is in the first place the extent of the stoplist. It is apparent that the more extended is this stoplist the less words are included into the index as keywords. Yet this dependence is not so simple, as the occurrence of the non-significant words in the titles plays an important part, too. Some conclusions can be drawn from the changes of the stoplist in the journal *Chemical Titles* which is the oldest journal using the KWIC index (Table 3.). Fig. 1 demonstrates that changes of the number of keywords per title do not strictly follow the changes in the extent of the stoplist.

Multiple alterations of the stoplist suggest the persistent effort of the editors of *Chemical Titles* to find the optimum extent and composition of this list. Every incorrectly included word can cause loss of important information in the index, and what is more, it is accompanied with higher requirements as to the machine time needed for searching the list. On the other hand, every word that was incorrectly not included in the list, increases the "noise" and the size of the index; this raises the production costs of the journal and the user is annoyed at stumbling over worthless keywords.

The considerable fluctuations in the views as to the selective value of some words are shown in Table 4. where in 32 selected words it is designated in which stoplists they were contained as non-significant. At the same time the same words appeared rather frequently in issues of *Chemical Titles* in which they were not considered non-significant, as e.g. in No. 11/1962 each of them appeared more than 10 times, the average being 25 times. The table does not allow to find out any striking regularity for determining the non-significance of these words and it is quite possible that the variance is, among others, due to different contexts in which the words appeared and which may have influenced their instantaneous significance.

The extents and contents of various other lists of non-significant words vary in a similar way and by comparison of half-a-dozen stoplists BRANDENBERG found only about two dozens of words which they had in common (5).

A short reference by EAST, SHAW and SMITH (6) prompted us to try to solve some of the above problems by means of direct designation of keywords in our input data. This modification saves in the first place expensive computing time and does not require too much human effort. Although we are not able to designate the keywords in 100 titles in 10 minutes, like EAST and coworkers, and need for it about three times as much time, the processing costs represent only about 1/10 of the costs required for automatic keyword selection by means of the computer.

Another important advantage of the modification lies in the possibility of not including among the keywords every actually non-significant word, however small its individual occurrence may be. Obviously, every set may contain quite a number of such sporadic words and including them systematically into the stoplist would lead to considerable and progressive enlargement of the list, resulting in continuous increase of the computer

WORDS	EXTENT OF STOPLIST									
	950	439	360	330	328	306	1153	1295	1319	1337
System, −S	N						N		N	N
Normal, Measurement, −S, Measuring, Octa							N	N	N	N
Natural, Industry	N							N	N	N
Characteristics, Research, Samples	N	N					N	N	N	N
Characterization	N	N	N				N	N	N	N
Formed	N	N	N	N			N	N	N	N
Active	N	N	N	N	N				N	N
Transfer	N	N	N	N	N				N	N
Control		N							N	N
Treatment, Rapid, Response							N	N	N	N
Solid, Light, Muscle, Resistance, Flow,									N	N
Radical, −S, Activities, Mixed, Ring, Heavy									N	N

time requirements. An attempt to demonstrate this problem in broader connections is given in Table 5. and 6. and in Fig. 2. analysing the situation in Vol. 3 No. 1 of *Index radiohygienicus.*

Table 5. Ratio (keywords/non-significant words) and (word types/occurrence in *Index radiohygienicus*, vol. 3, No. 1.

	WORD TYPES		OCCURRENCE		OCCURRENCE PER WORD
ONLY KEYWORDS	1442	69·3%	2977	33·2%	2·1
THE SAME WORDS AS KEYWORDS AND NON-SIG. WORDS	86	4·1%	587	6·6%	6·8
ONLY NON-SIG. WORDS	554	26·6%	5399	60·2%	9·7
ALL WORDS	2082	100%	8963	100%	4·3

Table 6. Distribution of non-significant words from *Index radiohygienicus*, vol. 3, No. 1.

	WORD TYPES		OCCURRENCE		OCCURRENCE PER WORD
ALL NON-SIG. WORDS	640	100%	5675	100%	8·8
STOPLIST C.TITLES	324	50·6%	4291	75·6%	13·2
BIOLOGICAL TERMS	54	8·5%	342	6·0%	6·3
RADIOLOGICAL TERMS	52	8·1%	655	11·5%	12·6
OTHER COMMON WORDS	210	32·8%	387	6·8%	1·8
SINGLY OCCURRING NON-SIG. WORDS	342	53·4%	342	6·0%	1·0

In the diagram the following facts can be seen, in particular:
1. the keywords represent only about 1/3 of all words in the titles, but about 2/3 of the whole vocabulary;
2. only one half of the words considered as non-significant could be found in the fullest stoplist used by the *Chemical Titles* and they naturally show the highest occurrence. If we do not take into account the biological and radiological non-significant terms typical for our specialized index, about 1/3 (210) of common non-significant words are left which should be included in the stoplist if we used it. Otherwise they would remain in the index as keywords with the total incidence of 387, extending the existing index by 12 per cent—which is not negligible;

3 more than one half of all non-significant words are those which appeared only once in the whole issue. The total number of all words in this particular issue of *Index radiohygienicus* being nearly 9,000, the occurrence of these words approaches the limit of 1:10,000 which at one time the editors of *Chemical Titles* considered decisive for not including a non-significant word into the stoplist. If we had not ommitted these singly occurring non-significant words, our index would have swollen by about 10 per cent. A similar situation was found in another issue (No. 4) of the same volume of *Index radiohygienicus*; moreover, it is very important that only 20 per cent of these singly occurring words had appeared in No. 1, too; the remaining 80 per cent (385) words would again significantly increase either the stoplist or the index;

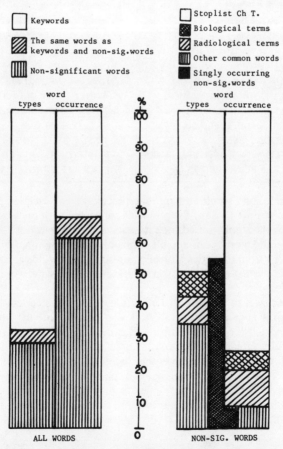

Fig. 2. Graphical representation of Tables 5. and 6.

4 86 words which appeared altogether 587 times were once considered as keywords, at another time as non-significant. This happened by mistake in a few cases only—such cases are practically the only weak point of the examined modification and this hazard can be substantially diminished by setting down the relevant instructions. In most cases the including of the same word in both groups is fully justified by the given context; this possibility is the third important advantage of the modification. The corresponding examples are given in Table 7.

Table 7. Examples of different significance of the same word.

NON SIGNIFICANT	SIGNIFICANT
NUCLEAR ENERGY	*NUCLEAR* PROTEINS
CRITICAL STUDY	*CRITICAL* ASSEMBLY
NUCLEAR POWER *PLANT*	*PLANT* TISSUES
HEALTH PHYSICS *DIVISION*	CELL *DIVISION*
GAMMA IRRADIATION	*GAMMA* SPECTROMETRY
WHOLE BODY IRRADIATION	*WHOLE BODY* COUNTER
TREATED WITH X-RAYS	*TREATED* WITH BONE MARROW
PROGRESS REPORT FOR *1965*	FALLOUT IN *1965*
NERVOUS *TISSUE*	*TISSUE* GRAFTING
DEVELOPMENT OF THE CHANGES	EMBRYONIC *DEVELOPMENT*
MILK SAMPLING *PROGRAM*	COMPUTER *PROGRAM*

In conclusion I would sum up that direct keyword selection proves to be able to remove most of the problems connected with the extent and content of the stoplists used for automatic keyword selection. Moreover, this procedure means considerable saving of computing time, enables us to leave out from the index all really non-significant words and makes it possible to evaluate the respective significance of the same word in different contexts.

As an answer to the potential objection that this is a certain step backward from the complex automatic indexing let me quote the words by Phyllis PARKINS from the Editorial Board of *Biological Abstracts* (8) which I fully agree with: "It is quite possible that it should be no longer said of all permuted-title indexes that their chief advantage is elimination of the creative work of human indexers, since we believe at present that a great advantage of the subject index to Biological Abstracts is its potential for using the creative work of skillful, biologically trained decidedly human editors."

REFERENCES:

1 HELBICH J.: 'Application of the KWIC—index in editing *Index radiohygienicus.*' Proc. Small Meeting Czech.Brit.Inform.Specialists, Liblice, May 16–21, 1966. Prague 1967 : 141–5.

2 LUHN H.P.: 'Automatic Creation of Literature Abstracts.' IBM J.Res.Develop. 2(2) : 160–5, 1958.

3 LUHN H.P.: 'Keyword-in-context index for technical literature (KWIC—index).' *Amer.Doc.* 11 (4) : 288–95, 1960.

4 STEVENS M.E.: 'Automatic indexing: A State-of-the-Art Report.' Washington: NBS Monograph 91, 1965 : 65.

5 BRANDENBERG W.: 'Write Titles for Machine Index Information Retrieval Systems.' *Automation and Scientific Communication, Short Papers,* Part 1 (Ed.H.P.Luhn). Washington 1963 : 57–8

6 EAST H., SHAW T.N., SMITH A.C.: 'Keyword-in-Context Indexes.' *Aslib Proc.* 15 (1) : 31–2, 1963.

7 FREEMAN R.R., DYSON M.D.: 'Development and Production of Chemical Titles, a current Awareness Index Publication prepared with the Aid of a Computer.' *J. Chem.Doc.* 3 (1) : 16–20, 1963.

8 PARKINS P.V.: 'Approaches to Vocabulary Management in Permuted Title Indexing of Biological Abstracts.' *Automation and Scientific Communication, Short Papers,* Part 1 (Ed. H.P.Luhn). Washington 1963 : 27–8

MEDLARS IN THE UNITED KINGDOM

E. S. PAGE

Computing Laboratory, University of Newcastle-upon-Tyne

Descriptions of MEDLARS (Medical Literature Analysis and Retrieval System) have been published in several places and for persons of different interests, (e.g. (1), (2), (3)). Briefly, the project is one mounted by the U.S. National Library of Medicine to assist in prompt publication of bibliographies of medical literature, particulary Index Medicus, and to make possible a Search Demand service for medical research workers. A substantial proportion of the world's medical literature is indexed—currently about 2,700 medical journals are covered in which about half the articles are in languages other than English. An article receives on average between 8 and 9 index terms taken from a list of Medical Subject Headings (MESH). MESH currently contains about 7,000 terms and is normally revised and enlarged as necessary each year. The indexers are, of course, not specialists in all of the topics mentioned by the articles but all have considerable training in the system itself and usually have graduate qualifications in a medical or related field. The indexing team spans some sixty languages.

In the indexing sequence, articles are distributed to indexers. checked by another qualified person and then key punched for input to the computer where a record on magnetic tape is created. The current rate of acquisitions is about 14,000 citations per month leading to a present file size of some half million citations packed into rather more than 100 M bytes on magnetic tape.

Attached to the Honeywell 800/200 computing system at the U.S. National Library of Medicine is a tape deck writing in IBM compatible format and each month IBM tapes with the new additions are despatched by air to the Computing Laboratory at the University of Newcastle-upon-Tyne to provide the file material for the Search Demand Service for the United Kingdom. The tapes have been made freely available by the N.L.M. for an experimental period and the development of the operational system has been supported by a grant from the Office of Scientific and Technical Information and staff and resources of the U.K. National Lending Library at Boston Spa. This service has been available to medical research workers in Britain since April 1966. Before that systems study and training of staff were undertaken. Miss E. D. Barraclough of the Computing Laboratory spent from March to June 1965 at Bethesda planning the computer aspects while Dr. Harley studied indexing and search techniques there. During the next nine months the basic search and file handling programmes were written for the English Electric KDF.9 computer. The configuration of this machine at Newcastle possesses 16,384 words of 48 bits each and four magnetic tape decks. The store (6μs cycle) and the logical operations (1μs in a nesting store) are rather faster than those of the N.L.M. system while the transfer rate between tapes and core is slower (40,000 characters/second). These machine characteristics make it advantageous to omit the preliminary coarse file search adopted a N.L.M. and to perform the necessary logical comparisons for the search in a single pass of the tape. Efficiency is increased by a rejection early in the logical comparison of citations not to be retrieved and, in this, the search formulators can assist once they have gained experience of the constitution of the file under the most important headings. The number of searches that can be run simultaneously in a batch is limited less by the size of core store than by the total time for a run. This time depends primarily on the number of terms that have to be looked at in a search expression before citations can be rejected and secondarily upon the number of citations retrieved. Program modifications have reduced the time for a batch of 10 searches of the computer file of "average complexity" (about 30 descriptors with logical connectives) to less than two hours. Searches on less than the complete file (e.g. those on the most recent month's tapes for a type of Selective Dissemination of Information service) occupy correspondingly less time or may be run in larger batches.

Between the start of routine search demand processing (13th May 1966) and the end of May 1967, the number of searches despatched was 1,007 and is currently running at about 100 searches per month. Of this total about 20% have originated in Newcastle University and the surrounding area (currently about 12% of new searches)—a high proportion compared with the fraction of the total national medical research activity (perhaps in the range 2–4%) which is due partly to the particular interest in MEDLARS shown by the University Medical School but principally we believe to the availability for discussion with the Research workers of a trained searcher in Newcastle. These figures may give some indication of the potential demand for searches in the country although they are likely to lead a considerable over-estimate of the actual demand at least in the first years of operation. Dr. Urquhart of the National Lending Library has pointed out that the U.S. experience of the number of searches after a longer establishment of the service is roughly that of the U.K. when due allowance is made for the relative volumes of medical research. The presence in a research centre of a trained searcher is, however, clearly significant and should be taken into account in subsequent planning.

During the operation so far of the U.K. MEDLARS service evaluation studies have been proceeding together with other research in information retrieval using the MEDLARS file as working material

Evaluation studies have been of different kinds, each nearing completion. Some searches despatched during the preliminary period have been accompanied by a request for information about the recipient's assessment of relevance from the titles. After sufficient time has elapsed for the output to be scrutinised about two-thirds of the users have replied showing the average proportion of articles judged relevant to their needs from the title to be of the order of 20%. The number of citations retrieved in a search varies from zero to several thousand, both extremes being experienced rarely and in special circumstances but the average is of the order of 300. Preliminary results of a survey of user attitudes by Miss. M. King indicates that about 75% of the research workers responding accept this bulk of citations as reasonable to scan by title and descriptors for possible relevance to their query. They go further and reject the suggestion of a smaller retrieval if the reduction would result in a loss of relevant referances. Half the searches failed to retrieve some relevant references previously known to be in the file but the value of the search was adjudged to be consequently decreased only to a minor extent by most users.

For all questions a manual search of Index Medicus and other bibliographic material would have been an alternative to the MEDLARS operation. Users estimated (or, perhaps, guessed) that an average of about six working days would be needed for a comparable manual search by the research worker or his assistant and rather less than half felt that such time could have been so spent.

A knowledge of the new references retrieved by the MEDLARS search was judged by about half the users to be a significant contribution to the research or practice. Although such users' views are necessarily subjective, are liable to bias from politeness or other reasons, and are difficult to quantify in monetary terms, the preliminary assessment must be that both money and time in substantial amounts are believed by the workers themselves to have been saved. When the survey is complete, Miss King will prepare a more detailed description and evaluation of it.

At a more fundamental level methods of evaluation themselves have been considered and MEDLARS searches used as examples. Methods of evaluation not dependent upon a comparison of systems have used measures like "recall" and "precision", the former of which is impractical to measure in a large file. A different measure formed from the ratio of the number of relevant references known after the search to the number known before has been suggested by W. L. Miller and evidence, both theoretical and practical, produced to show how slight is the dependence upon a user's knowledge or temperament.

Procedures devised by W. L. Miller for ordering a retrieval in order of an estimated likelihood of relevance have been investigated and are being applied to alternative forms of search strategy on the MEDLARS file. A single comparison of a MEDLARS search with a manual one performed in a total of sixteen hours by librarians using Index Medicus and other bibliographic and abstract sources has been reported by Dr. Harley (Table 1). Two striking features are a) the number of relevant articles in Index

Medicus missed by the manual search and b) articles in Index Medicus (and so in the Medlars file) not retrieved by the search as formulated.

Table 1. Comparison Of Machine And Manual Searches

Articles	Machine only	Both	Manual only
Retrieved	116	20	67
Relevant	57	16	61
In Index Medicus	116	20	18
Relevant	57	16	17

The repetitive searches on the current file are

The repetitive searches on the current file are being used to test methods of automatic improvement of searches. W. A. Gray and W. L. Miller have constructed a limited citation file of about 3,000 documents giving references to and from each other in a specialised area of medicine using as basis the manual card-file maintained by a Medical Research Council Unit. This file will be used both for comparisons of search strategy and for investigations of some semi-automatic indexing techniques.

The work in information retrieval at Newcastle is distinct from that currently being undertaken into the conversion of existing library catalogues into computer readable form, the mechanisation of library procedures, the work on linked records and computer typesetting but naturally complements them.

REFERENCES:

1 THE MEDLARS STORY: 'N.L.M.' U.S. Department of Health, Education and Welfare. (1965).

2 A. J. HARLEY: 'U.K. MEDLARS: A Handbook for Users'. N.L.L. Boston Spa. (1966).

3 A. J. HARLEY AND E. D. BARRACLOUGH. 'MEDLARS Information Retrieval in Britain'. *Postgrad.Med.J.* 42, (February 1966) No. 484, 69–73.

APPENDIX

In the period between speaking about MEDLARS at the Symposium and the decision to prepare proceedings for publications, many developments have taken place in the MEDLARS operation in Britain and the work in information retrieval in Newcastle.

The routine processing of MEDLARS searches is now performed principally at the Documentation Processing Centre and a smaller number at Newcastle, both using the Newcastle programs.

MEDLARS Liaison Officers, stationed in different parts of the country have been appointed and trained as searchers, of whom Miss King has become one and thus extends the role she played mainly for the Newcastle region during the experimental period. All these searchers supplement the work of Dr. Harley and his colleagues at N.L.L. and are coordinated by him.

The assessments of the value of the retrieval scheme mentioned at the Seminar as being in progress have been completed (reference A.1). The theoretical work on comparative assessments of retrieval strategies and the practical results using the MEDLARS File and user population by W. L. Miller are in final draft form for this thesis. The semi-automatic searching and indexing techniques studied by W. A. Gray are in a similar state and form the basis for work supported by a new O.S.T.I. research grant using an on-line inter-active computer.

REFERENCE:

A.1 M. KING: Report on the Operation of the MEDLARS Service in the Newcastle Region from 1966–1968. January 1969.

THE CHEMICAL SOCIETY RESEARCH UNIT IN INFORMATION DISSEMINATION AND RETRIEVAL: AN EXPERIMENT IN COMPUTER—BASED CHEMICAL INFORMATION RETRIEVAL

A. K. KENT

Chemical Society Research Unit in Information Dissemination and Retrieval, University of Nottingham

INTRODUCTION

There are few who would deny that, with the ever increasing output of scientific literature, there is an urgent need to investigate all the possible ways in which access by individual scientists to the results of research, bearing on their own work, may be improved. The Chemical Society, in closest collaboration with the Chemical Abstracts Service (CAS) of the American Chemical Society, and with the Office for Scientific and Technical Information (OSTI) of the Department of Education and Science, established, in August 1966, a "Research Unit in Information Dissemination and Retrieval". The Unit was formed at the University of Nottingham by the appointment of a Director and a Systems Programmer—its initial objectives were to investigate the value, relative to existing means, for users of chemical information in the United Kingdom, of searching, by computer, the magnetic tape versions of the CAS publications *Chemical Titles* (CT) and *Chemical Biological Activities* (CBAC). A current—awareness service was to be provided, without charge, to selected closed—populations of chemists who, in return, would assist the Unit in the evaluation of the service.

By mid-January 1967 the Unit had produced an operational computer search system for the English-Electric Leo Marconi KDF9, which was available to us at the University of Nottingham, and since that time a regular fortnightly literature—alerting service has been provided to about two hundred and sixty individual scientists from fourteen University and Government institutions and Industrial organisations. These first few months have, inevitably, been spent in refining and improving the original computer system, and in acquiring, and passing on to our users, a better understanding of the way to use such a service. Relatively little evaluation of the service has yet been possible; however, the computer programs are now operating satisfactorily, and our understanding of the processes of "profile" construction are such that we believe that it will be possible to begin a serious study of the value of these services by not later than mid-July 1967.

In this paper we shall describe the CT/CBAC service from our own and from the user's point of view, but concentrating attention particularly on those processes which present most difficulty to a user familiar only with conventional methods of information retrieval. A number of tables and charts are appended, and serve to amplify points which are dealt with in little detail, or not at all, in the text. In a final section we shall briefly review some other present, and possible future activities of the Unit.

THE SERVICE PROVIDED (see Figure 1)

The CAS CT and CBAC tapes reach the Unit at fortnightly intervals. Each issue of CT contains the titles of four-five thousand papers (as well as standard bibliographic information—see Table 1 for details of CT and CBAC tape formats) taken from about seven hundred and fifty journals. Each issue of CBAC contains the titles, and a descriptive digest, of about five hundred papers relating to:

(i)   The action of chemical compounds on biological systems
(ii) The activities of chemical compounds in biological systems
(iii) The *in vitro* activities of biologically significant chemical compounds, and taken from about five hundred and fifty journals.

User's question ("profiles") are matched against one or other, or both tapes as desired, and the resulting "hits" dispatched as soon as possible after the run. The types of output available are described in Appendix 1.

After inspection of the output the user may, if he wishes, instruct the Unit to make amendments to his profile prior to the next run. There is no retrospective element in the service, so there is no possibility of later retrieving papers missed because of an inadequate profile. It is, therefore, of the greatest importance that the profiles be carefully designed from the start, and, if they are inadequate initially, that they be quickly amended and improved.

PREPARING THE SEARCH PROFILE (see Figure 2)

At all stages in the preparation of a search profile there is one point which must be constantly borne in mind—the data that is being searched is in the form of "free text", and there is no control over the modes of expression that may be used by the author in writing his title, or the digest-writer in preparing the digest. The user must attempt to anticipate *all* possible modes of expression if he is to capture all relevant information. We shall see in a moment how the profile writer may at least approach, if not achieve, this ideal.

a) The original question. The user's first task is to describe, in his own words, the field of his interest. It is often the case that a particular field of interest cannot conveniently be covered by a single question—if so it should be divided into several questions, each pertaining to one well-

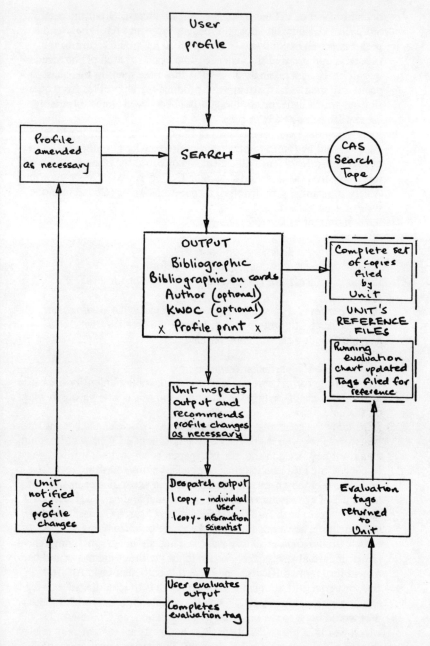

Fig. 1.

defined aspect of the more general field of interest. Often the need for more than one question does not become apparent until the user has progressed well beyond this first step—if so he should return to the first step, and proceed through each step again for each of the several questions. It is increasingly clear to us that time spent in this phase is profitably spent—most attempts to produce search profiles from questions to which little, or no, thought has been given almost invariably cause difficulties at a later stage.

b) Identifying the essential elements in the question. Any properly framed question will be found to break down into usually not more than three or four separately identifiable elements or concepts. If more are found it is likely that the question should be treated as two or more questions. A very substantial proportion of all questions we handle fall into one type of general form:—

the *activities* of a *class of compounds*

or

the *properties* of a *class of compounds*

A more complex question might have the form:—

the *action* of a *class of compounds* in a *class of organisms*

or

the *properties* of a *class of compounds* in a particular *environment*

It is less usual, but quite possible, to have the forms:—

anything about a *class of compounds*

or

anything about a particular *technique*

Whatever the form, however, it should be possible to identify the basic elemental concepts within the question, and this is vital before moving on the next phase.

c) Expanding the concepts. Once identified the basic elements of the question must be viewed in the light of the question:— "What words would an author have used in the title of a paper, or an abstractor in a digest to convey the idea implicit in each concept in my question". At this point the user may need considerable help in expanding each concept into a list of synonyms, related terms, broader and narrower terms. CAS have produced, both for CT and for CBAC, "Search Guides" which, in large measure, serve this function. A sample page from one of these Search Guides appears as Appendix 2. They are not, as yet, comprehensive or indeed always entirely accurate, but without them it would be a great deal more difficult to perform this particular task. An alternative, or better still, supplementary approach is to scan the titles or digests of a reasonable sample, if such is available, of papers which the user would hope to see retrieved by his question, and to determine which words or phrases in these titles or digests are semantically related to each of the concepts in his question. This process may, incidentally, have a salutary effect on his own future efforts at titling research papers as he realizes the failure of many titles to give any indication what-

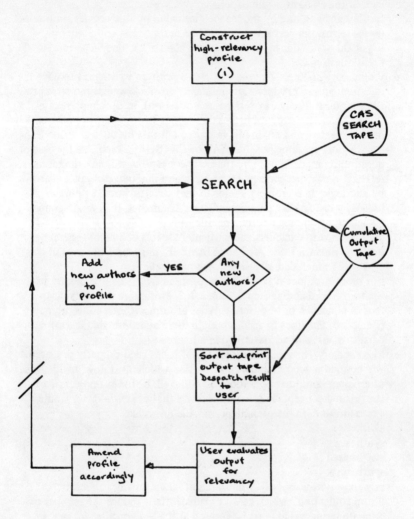

(1)   The original profile should consist of terms which will only capture relevant information – author names will probably form a large part

Fig. 2

ever of the content of the paper.

By these means, and by the recall, stimulated by this activity, of other useful terms, the user should produce a more or less comprehensive list of the variations in mode of expression for each concept contained in his question.

d) Preliminary coding. The user is now in a position to attempt to code his question, and to produce a preliminary "profile" (we use the term profile to refer to the coded version of a question). In the simplest case this will consist merely of listing the various words and/or phrases which he has selected, and linking them one to another by the use of the Boolean logical operator *or*. Thus CAT *or* CATS *or* FELINE. In the case of questions comprised of more than one concept he will link the terms relating to any one concept by *or* logic, and link one concept to another by *and* logic. In a profile we refer to these lists of words or phrases linked by *or* logic as "parameters". One parameter, or several parameters linked by *and* logic form a profile. It is possible to use the logical operator *not* to exclude some particular aspects of a more general query:— thus CAT *or* CATS *not* SIAMESE. In general all terms of this type will be included in a single "*not* parameter".

For most questions it is possible to proceed from this preliminary profile to the final coding step. In some, however, more subtle associations of concepts, or of different types of term within a concept, may be needed. Facilities to accommodate these questions are, at least in part, available and are described in a later section.

e) Final coding. The preliminary profile, if it has been properly prepared, will contain much redundant information which must now, for the sake of efficient computer operation, be removed. If, for example, one of the original concepts in the question was that of *synthesis* we would expect to find, in the preliminary profile terms like:

synthesise
synthesises
synthesised
synthetic

as well as synthesis itself. Our search program provides a facility for "term truncation" which can very substantially reduce the number of separate terms which must be entered in the final profile. We can reduce the list above to the single term:

SYNTHE*

where the asterisk is interpreted to mean "accept any character or characters in this position, including a space". Asterisks may be used both as prefixes or suffixes or both. Thus:

SYNTHE

would capture also:—

photosynthetic
biosynthesis
and so on.

The term truncation facility is not without its dangers. It is very easy to fall into the trap of using a truncated term to substitute for several terms without realizing that it will also serve to capture other terms of no interest. Thus cat, cats might be truncated to CAT*—needless to say the results would be *cat*astrophic! It is often very difficult to guess at the effects of term truncation, especially if the term is truncated both at front and back—but the facility is so useful that we have produced in the Unit an aid to the choice of appropriate truncations which we call a Keyletter-in-Context (or KLIC) Index. A sample page appears as Appendix 3. A truncated term can be compared with this Index, and a list of all the words which would be captured by it, together with their relative frequencies in a number of issues of CT and /or CBAC, can be quickly obtained. With this device to aid him the user can be quite confident, by adjusting the term appropriately, that his truncated term is not going to capture large amounts of unwanted, irrelevant information. It is important, in this final coding phase, to check on spellings and conventions adopted by CAS in preparation of their CT/CBAC Search Tapes. Both CAS and the Unit produce, or are about to produce, word frequency listings in which spelling and abbreviation conventions can be checked. These lists also serve to give the user some indication of the numbers of titles likely to be captured by each of the search terms in his profile, and facilitate the making of intelligent decisions regarding the choice of terms to allow expansion or restriction of the scope of the profile.

Stages a—d will normally only be followed during the initial framing of a question for our service (unless very substantial changes in an already existing profile need to be made). This step of final coding, however, will often be taken by the user who wishes to adjust his profile to improve its retrieval efficiency, or to take account of changes in emphasis in his own interests. Output from previous searches with a profile are thus, in a sense, a further aid to the user in more closely defining his question, and in helping to ensure that a minimum of relevant information is missed, and a minimum of irrelevant information is retrieved.

f) The use of weights. Our experience is that weights provide a useful form of conditional logic, as well as possibly serving to arrange output in some sort of order of interest. The use of weights is best illustrated by an example of each possible application.

A user is interested in discovering information relating to deformities in dogs of any breed; for breeds other than bulldogs, however, he wishes to be alerted only to articles on congenital deformities. A weighted search as follows would achieve this result:

PARAMETER 1   BULLDOGS   weight 10
                     or BULLDOG   10
                     or DOG   5
                     or DOGS   5

and

PARAMETER 2   DEFORM*   5

and

PARAMETER 3   CONGENITAL   5

Threshold weight = 15

In our implementation of weights we sum the highest weight term scoring a "hit" from each parameter, compare this with the threshold weight, and record a "hit" for the profile if the sum of term weights is equal to, or greater than the threshold weight. The *and* logic does *not* have to be satisfied in weighted searches. Thus the title:

"Deformities in the bulldog"

is a hit (sum of term weights 10 + 5 = 15)

though:

"Deformities in seven breeds of dog"

is not (sum of term weights 5 + 5 = 10).

We are a little doubtful of the value of weights in arranging output from searches in some sort of "interest rank". However, it is possible so to order output if desired. Thus if, taking another version of the question described above, the user is more interested in deformities in certain breeds and less in others, a suitable scale of weights can be used to organize output in question weight order.

Negative weights may be used in place of *not* logic, and are often preferable since their effect is not necessarily so absolute. A user might wish to be alerted to papers describing the effect of alcohol on vision in mammals other than man. The search:

ALCOHOL

and

EFFECT* *or* ACTION* *or* INFLUENCE*

and

MAMMAL* *or* RAT *or* RATS *or* RABBIT* *or* GUINEA PIG*

not

MAN

could lead to the exclusion of papers of the type:

"A comparison of the effects of alcohol on vision in mammals other than man".

By selection of suitable weights many such mistaken exclusions can be avoided.

THE SEARCH PROGRAM

a) Items which may be used as search terms. In Table 1 are summarized the CT and CBAC tape formats, and an indication is given of the items contained on the tapes which are available for searching.

  (i) Title or text. Any string of characters up to about sixty characters in length, which may include spaces, punctuation marks etc., may be requested as a search term for matching against titles

(CT and CBAC), or digest text (CBAC). For example:—

NUCLEAR MAGNETIC RESONANCE

2,4-DICHLOROPHENOXYACETIC ACID

Title or text terms may be truncated, as described earlier.

(ii) Author names. Author surnames alone, or surnames with initials may be specified.

(iii) Journal coden. The ASTM coden for journals may be used to select or, more commonly to exclude certain journals from consideration.

(iv) Registry number. In CBAC all compounds mentioned in the digest are tagged with the CAS Compound Registry Number. These numbers may be specified as search terms, and can be very valuable in cases where a compound of interest has many trivial or trade names, but can be unambiguously identified by the Registry Number.

(v) Molecular formula. The molecular formula, like the Registry Number, is available on CBAC, and may be used for searching. In practice we find this facility relatively little used.

b) The computer program. The flow chart for the computer system is presented in Figure 4. A detailed description of the program is in preparation, and will be published as soon as possible.

c) Search statistics. Table 2 presents some statistics of our search program based on our experiences during the four months January - April 1967 with about two hundred and sixty users in the CT/CBAC experiment.

d) Output formats. Samples of the output formats made available to our users are illustrated in Appendix 1. The basic output format is the conventional bibliographic listing—each search "hit" is output in the form of the title of the paper, author's name/s, journal name, volume and pagination. These listings are produced on continuous line-printer stationery, and on "tab"-cards. The cards, which have a small tear-off tag attached to each, are apparently extremely popular with our users, since they may be conveniently filed for future reference in a conventional card index. The tear-off tags are pre-printed with a set of queries relating to the relevance or otherwise of the title in question; on completion by the user these are returned to the Unit to form the basis for our evaluation of the service.

Many users have found that a form of output which we have described as a Keyword-out-of-Context Index (KWOC) is a valuable aid to them. In this format the title, and a compressed bibliographic entry of each "hit" is listed under each of the profile search terms contained in the title, or, in the case of CBAC, in the title and digest. This form of output has proved useful, on the one hand to CBAC users where many of the "hits" to which they are alerted are captured by search terms present only in the digest, and from whose titles it is often uncertain why a hit was ever recorded, and on the other hand to both CT and CBAC users in providing a convenient indication of the effectiveness of par-

ticular search terms in capturing information of interest.
An author listing is also optionally available, but very little requested.

Table 1 Search Statistics

	CT	CBAC
Number of Profiles	395	187
Number of Terms	8272	4179
Terms/Profile	c21	c22½
Smallest Profile	1 term	1 term
Largest Profile	283 terms	234 terms
Number of Profiles Using Weights	52 (13%)	29 (16%)
Number of Profiles Using *NOT* Logic	108 (27%)	44 (24%)
Number of Profiles With: —		
1 Parameter	105	60
2 Parameters	189	86
3 Parameters	84	32
> 3 Parameters	17	9*
Computer Times Search	c 3 hours	c 1 hour
Profile Amend and Compilation	c 20 minutes	c 10 minutes
Sort and Print	c 2½ hours	c 1¼ hours
Estimated Total Computer Cost Per Search Term/		
Search (at full commercial rate of	2/9d.	2/3d.
£187-10-0d. per hour = c $500	c 35 cents	c 30 cents**
Mean Computer Cost/Profile/Annum		
	£78	£68
	$220	$190

*n.b. These are almost all weighted searches (see later).

** Printing time is charged at full rate, but, of course, could and should be done off-line.

Table 1 CT/CBAC Tape Formats

Type of Information	Occurs on Search Tape		Available for Searching		Search Term Type	COMMENTS
	CT	CBAC	CT	CBAC		
Title	YES	YES	YES	YES	T	On CT a substantial number of words, especially chemical compound names, are fragmented to improve KWIC Indexing. Foreign language titles are translated, and spelling Americanised.
Author Name	YES	YES	YES	YES	A	
Journal Name	YES	YES	YES	YES	C	In the form of ASTM Coden.
Volume or Issue Number	YES	YES	NO	NO		Has doubtful value for current-awareness searching.
Date of Publication	NO	YES	NO	NO		Only the YEAR is given —of doubtful value for current-awareness searching in any event.
Institution Address	NO	YES	NO	NO		Could be of value if available for searching.
Digest	NO	YES	NO	YES	T	A digest of from 50 to several 100 words is available for searching on CBAC.
CAS Compound Registry Numbers	NO	YES	NO	YES	R	Each compound mentioned in the digest is identified also by its CAS Compound Registry Number (CBAC).
Molecular Formula	NO	YES	NO	YES	M	A molecular formula for each compound mentioned is available for searching on the CBAC tape.

GENERAL REMARKS

All characters on the tape are represented by the IBM printer set-consequently there is no discrimination between upper and lower case alphabetic characters, Greek symbols are replaced by Roman and certain punctuation marks altered.

Table 2. Relevance vs. Search Output For Sample CT and CBAC Runs

No. of Hits	CT RELEVANCE					CBAC RELEVANCE				
	<10%	10-25%	26-50%	>00%		<10%	10-25%	26-50%	>50%	
<10	16	6	6	26	54	19	6	8	13	46
	30%	11%	11%	48%		41%	13%	17%	29%	
10-25	4	7	9	11	31	7	4	12	11	34
	13%	23%	30%	34%		21%	12%	35%	32%	
26-50	2	13	10	9	34	1	2	4	5	12
	6%	38%	29%	27%		8%	17%	33%	42%	
51-100	2	3	2	1	8					
	25%	37%	25%	13%						
>100	1	2	1	1	5				1	1
	20%	40%	20%	20%					100%	
	25	31	28	48	132	27	12	24	30	93
	19%	23%	21%	37%		29%	13%	26%	32%	

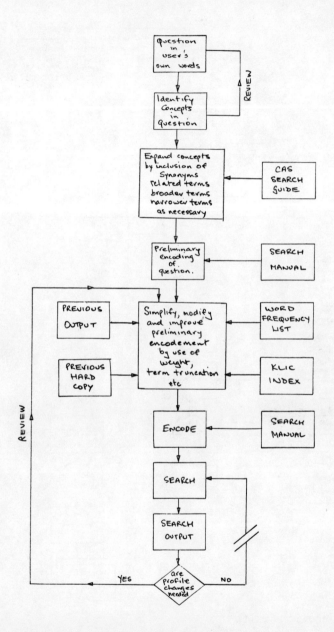

Fig. 3 Profile Construction and Maintenance

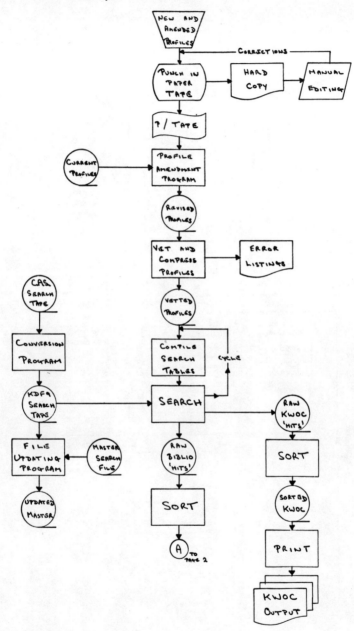

Fig. 4 Author Searches (1)

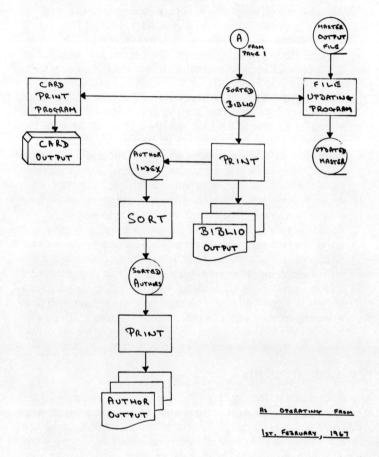

Fig. 4 Author Searches (2)

FEEDBACK

The Unit receives feedback from users in a variety of ways.

(i)   Profile maintenance. The search output from each run is accom-
        panied by a print-out of the user's current profile (see Appendix
        4). Members of the Unit inspect some or all of the output prior
        to despatch and, if necessary, note on this print-out possibly ben-
        eficial profile modications. The user, after receiving his output,
        may mark his own profile modications on this sheet. On return to
        the Unit the annotated profile print-out forms the basis for the
        preparation of a profile amendment tape which is input prior to
        each search (see Figure 3).

(ii)   Tear-off evaluation tags. A sample of card output, with its assoc-
        iated tear-off evaluation tag is attached. Completed tags are re-
        turned by the user to the Unit and filed. They will form the basis
        for the detailed evaluation which we are presently beginning;
        meanwhile, however, they serve as a useful routine check on pro-
        file performance, and in particular, in drawing to our attention
        profiles which consistently produce very high or very low rele-
        vance. These profiles are given attention, and the cause for the
        abnormal relevance figures removed, if this is possible.

(iii)   Personal contact. A member of the Unit visits each group of users
        involved in the experiment at least once every eight-nine weeks to
        discuss particular problems, and to answer queries regarding the
        service which may arise from time to time. This personal contact
        is most important in establishing and maintaining the user's con-
        fidence in the service provided, and provides the Unit with a val-
        uable opportunity to assess the subjective factors which may in-
        fluence users in their acceptance, or otherwise, of a computer-
        based current-awareness service of this kind.

FUTURE DEVELOPMENTS

We may safely claim that by May 1967 the Unit was operating CT and
CBAC current-awareness searches on a routine basis, and that most of the
early difficulties have been solved. For the next year we shall attempt to
evaluate the services to determine relevance, and recall, and to relate these
to types of profile, and types of user. A detailed description of our proposed techniques will be published in the near future, and the final results towards the end of 1968.

Our next immediate step is to begin programming for retrospective
searching. We propose to develop a comprehensive system which, in addition to providing programs for retrospective and current-awareness* information tools (e.g., a "New Word Alert"), and guide to questioners
(e.g., Word Frequency Lists, KLIC Indexes). The system will centre on a
set of inverted files in which substantial file compression will be achieved
so as to improve tape search times. Use of disc-files will be introduced,

and many additional facilities provided for the user. Of particular value will be the facility to specify contextual associations of search terms. *searching of CAS magnetic tapes, will provide additional

ACKNOWLEDGMENTS

The Unit is indebted to the Chemical Society, and the Office for Scientific and Technical Information of the Department of Education and Science for financial support, and to Chemical Abstracts Service, Columbus, Ohio, for unfailing generosity in provision of search tapes, and much else besides. Last, but by no means least, the Unit wishes to take this opportunity to thank our collaborators in this experiment for their patience during our early faltering steps into this field.

K

RUN AGAINST   BIBLIOGRAPHIC LISTING OF REFERENCES FOR PROFILE NO. 016

CHEMICAL-BIOLOGICAL ACTIVITIES   VOLUME 05   ISSUE 01   ON 14/01/67

```
        STASON WB              CANNON PJ          HEINEMANN HO
        LARAGH JH
        FUROSEMIDE.B
        A CLINICAL EVALUATION OF ITS DIURETIC ACTION.B
        JOURNAL CIRC-A    VOLUME 34 (1966)    ISSUE 5   PAGES 910-20
        CBAC DIGEST NO. 143            ARTICLE WEIGHT 0


        ZAHN RK            TIEGLER E        HEICKE B
        HANSKE W        FORSTER W       ET AL.
        CELLULAR DIVISION AND CELLULAR VOLUME DISTRIBUTION IN THE
        PRESENCE OF 2-PHENYLETHANOL AND SOME OF ITS DERIVATIVES.B
        JOURNAL NATU-A    VOLUME 211 (1966)   ISSUE 5059   PAGES 298-
        CBAC DIGEST NO. 329            ARTICLE WEIGHT 0
```

        2 BIBLIOGRAPHIC REFERENCES PRODUCED FOR PROFILE NO. 016

Appendix 1

RUN AGAINST   CHEMICAL-BIOLOGICAL ACTIVITIES   VOLUME 05   ISSUE 01

KEYWORD-OUT-OF-CONTEXT (KWOC) INDEX FOR PROFILE NO. 016

ON 14/01/67

CHLOR

CELLULAR DIVISION AND CELLULAR VOLUME DISTRIBUTION IN THE
PRESENCE OF 2-PHENYLETHANOL AND SOME OF ITS DERIVATIVES.*
JOURNAL NATU-A   STARTING PAGE 298

ETHAN

CELLULAR DIVISION AND CELLULAR VOLUME DISTRIBUTION IN THE
PRESENCE OF 2-PHENYLETHANOL AND SOME OF ITS DERIVATIVES.*
JOURNAL NATU-A   STARTING PAGE 298

FLUOR

CELLULAR DIVISION AND CELLULAR VOLUME DISTRIBUTION IN THE
PRESENCE OF 2-PHENYLETHANOL AND SOME OF ITS DERIVATIVES.*
JOURNAL NATU-A   STARTING PAGE 298

C 0024H 00320 0045 001

FUROSEMIDE.*
A CLINICAL EVALUATION OF ITS DIURETIC ACTION.*
JOURNAL CIRC-A   STARTING PAGE 910

4 KEYWORD REFERENCES PRODUCED FOR PROFILE NO. 016

Appendix 1

RUN AGAINST   CHEMICAL-BIOLOGICAL ACTIVITIES   VOLUME 05   ISSUE 05

AUTHOR INDEX LISTING OF REFERENCES FOR PROFILE NO. 002   ON 15/03/67

CHERMANN JC	JOURNAL	AIPX=A	STARTING PAGE 70
DIGEON M	JOURNAL	AIPX=A	STARTING PAGE 70
GROBECKER H	JOURNAL	APEP=A	STARTING PAGE 474
GUYOT=JEANNIN N	JOURNAL	AIPX=A	STARTING PAGE 70
HOLTZ P	JOURNAL	APEP=A	STARTING PAGE 474
JB	JOURNAL	MURE=A	STARTING PAGE 90
JENKINS	JOURNAL	MURE=A	STARTING PAGE 90
MUELLER HK	JOURNAL	APEP=A	STARTING PAGE 474
PARISH DJ	JOURNAL	BJCA=A	STARTING PAGE 200
RAYNAUD M	JOURNAL	AIPX=A	STARTING PAGE 70
SEARLE CE	JOURNAL	BJCA=A	STARTING PAGE 200
SONDHI KC	JOURNAL	PNAS=A	STARTING PAGE 1743
TUROCZI LJ	JOURNAL	PNAS=A	STARTING PAGE 1743

13 AUTHOR INDEX REFERENCES PRODUCED FOR PROFILE NO. 002

Appendix 1

CAST IRONS   (CONT)   CASTOR OIL
    RT CARBON STEELS   BT OILS
    RT CASTING ALLOYS
    RT CASTINGS   CASTOR-OIL PLANT
    RT GRAPHITIZATION   BT HERBS
    RT MELTING   BT PLANT (BIOLOGICAL)
    RT PEARLITE   SY RICINUS COMMUNIS
    RT STEADITE
                                                   CASTRATION
CAST PRODUCTS (FOR REMELTING)   NT EMASCULATION
    BT CASTING   NT GELDING
    RT ALLOYS   NT OOPHORECTOMY
                                                       NT SPAYING
CAST PRODUCTS (FOR REWORKING)   RT EUNUCH
    BT CASTING   RT FEMINIZATION
    RT ALLOYS   RT OVARY
                                                       RT STERILITY
CASTING   RT STERILIZATION
    NT BRONZE CASTINGS   RT TESTIS
    NT CAST FORGING STOCK   RT WETHER
    NT CAST PRODUCTS (FOR REMELTING)   SY ORCHIECTOMY
    NT CAST PRODUCTS (FOR REWORKING)
    NT DIE CASTINGS   CAT
    NT EXTRUSION INGOTS   S* FELIS CATUS
    NT FOUNDRY INGOTS
    NT INGOTS   CATABOLISM
    NT PIGS   BT METABOLISM
    NT ROLLING INGOTS   SY DESTRUCTIVE METABOLISM
    NT SOWS   SY KATABOLISM
    NT STEEL CASTINGS
    NT T-INGOTS   CATALASE
    NT TITANIUM CASTINGS   BT ENZYMES
    NT WIRE BAR
    RT ALLOYS   CATALEPSY
    RT BILLETS   RT CATALEPTIC AGENTS
    RT BLOWHOLES
    RT CAST ALUMINUM ALLOYS   CATALEPTIC AGENTS
    RT CAST COPPER ALLOYS   RT CATALEPSY
    RT CAST IRONS   SY CATALEPTICS
    RT CASTING
    RT CASTING ALLOYS   CATALEPTICS
    RT COLUMNAR STRUCTURE   S* CATALEPTIC AGENTS
    RT DEFECTS
    RT DEGASSING   CATALYSIS
    RT FORGING   NT AUTO-CATALYSIS
    RT GATES   RT ACCELERATING (PROCESS)
    RT INCLUSIONS   RT ACCELERATION(CHEMICAL)
    RT LIQUID METALS   RT ACTIVATION
    RT MELTING   RT ACTIVITY(CHEMICAL)
    RT METALLURGY   RT ARRESTING (PROCESS)
    RT MICROSTRUCTURE   RT CATALYSTS
    RT MILL PRODUCTS   RT CATALYTIC CRACKING
    RT MOLDINGS   RT CATALYTIC REFORMING
    RT MOLDS   RT INHIBITION
    RT PINHOLES   RT MECHANISMS (REACTION)
    RT PRODUCT DESIGN   RT ORTHO-PARA CONVERSION
    RT RISERS   RT PHOTOSYNTHESIS
    RT SEMIFABRICATED PRODUCTS   RT PROCESSING
    RT SOLIDIFICATION   RT REACTIONS (CHEMICAL)
    RT SPRUES   RT RETARDING
    SY GATING(CASTING)   RT STABILIZATION
                                                       RT STABILIZING
CASTING ALLOYS   RT SURFACE CHEMISTRY
    RT CAST IRONS   RT SYNTHESIS
    RT CASTING
    RT LIQUID METALS   CATALYST BASE
    RT MELT   RT SUBSTRATES

CASTING STEELS   CATALYST CIRCULATION
    BT STEELS   BT CIRCULATION

CASTLE'S INTRINSIC FACTOR   CATALYSTS
    S* INTRINSIC FACTORS   NT ANTIOXIDANT
                                                       NT COCATALYSTS

Appendix 2

KWIC INDEX

PAGE 4

Appendix 3

PROFILE NO. 002   MASTER/EXPERIMENTAL

RUN 15/03/67 AGAINST CHEMICAL BIOLOGICAL ACTIVITIES   VOL. 05   ISSUE 05

PARAMETER	TYPE	LOGIC	WEIGHT	TERM
01	T	AND		*MELAN*
01	T	OR		*CHROMATOPH*
01	T	OR		*ERITHROPH*
01	T	OR		*XANTHOPHO*
01	T	OR		*LEUCOPH*
01	T	OR		*INTERMEDIN*
01	T	OR		INTERMEDIATE LOBE
01	T	OR		PARS INTERMEDIA
01	T	OR		METADENCHYPOPHYSIS
01	T	OR		*MSH*
01	T	OR		*M.S.H*
01	T	OR		*MELANOCYTE*STIMULAT*
01	T	OR		*MELANOCYTE STIMULAT*

OUTPUT FORMATS REQUESTED   BIBLIO KWOC AUTHOR

REQUESTED OUTPUT ENCLOSED/NO OUTPUT ON THIS RUN

PLEASE COMPLETE EVALUATION FORM/EVALUATION TAGS AND RETURN AS SOON AS POSSIBLE TO THE RESEARCH UNIT

IF CHANGES TO THIS PROFILE ARE REQUIRED PLEASE MARK THEM ON THIS FORM IN THE FOLLOWING WAY
     DELETE ENTIRE TERMS OR PARAMETERS BY STRIKING THEM OUT CLEARLY
     ADD NEW TERMS OR PARAMETERS IN THE SPACE PROVIDED = OR ON THE REVERSE IF MORE SPACE IS NEEDED
     MARK CHANGES TO TYPE/LOGIC/WEIGHTS/OUTPUT FORMATS BY DELETION OR INSERTION OR BOTH APPROPRIATELY
     AND RETURN IT TO US AS SOON AS POSSIBLE

PLEASE NOTE THAT CHANGES SHOULD NOT BE MADE IN A MASTER PROFILE UNLESS THE EFFECT OF THE PROPOSED CHANGES
HAS BEEN INVESTIGATED THOROUGHLY IN AN EXPERIMENTAL PROFILE.

Appendix 4

INDEX